MEAT-FREE

One Pound Meals

PHOTOGRAPHY
DAN JONES

DESIGN
SUPERFANTASTIC

MEAT-FREE

One Pound Meals

www.miguelbarclay.com

CONTENTS

You'll know by now that there are no chapters in my *One Pound Meals* books.
Either flick through and choose something that takes your fancy
or pick a dish from this handy list.

Welcome 9

Meat-Free Challenge 10

The Principles Behind One Pound Meals 12

Apple & Stilton Slaw 144

Aubergine Milanese 76

Aubergine Pangrattato 190

Aubergine Parmigiana 160

Aubergine Pho 170

Aubergine Ragu & Polenta 194

Aubergine Thermidor 130

Beetroot Latkes 116

Bell Pepper Jalfrezi 198

Black Bean & Chilli Enchiladas 22

Black Bean Moussaka 96

Blinis 132

Butternut Squash Polenta 156

Cabbage Potstickers 102

Cacio e Pepe 56

Cannellini Beans with Leek & Tomatoes 54

Caponata 110

Caramelised Onion Quiche 158

Carrot & Coriander Salad 106

Cashews in Black Bean Sauce 114

Cauliflower Tacos 78

Cauliflower 3 ways 86

Chana Masala 138

Charred Peppers & Breadcrumbs 134

Cheese Soufflé Omelette 112

Chickpea & Saag Mash 142

Chinese-Style Oyster Mushrooms 84

Chunky Balti Veg Pie 192

Coconut Daal 162

Coronation Chickpeas 94

Crispy Potato Caesar Salad 184

Feta Goujons 74

Filo Bianco 174

French Toast 16

Fried Tomatoes & Courgettes 180

Green Bean & Lentil Curry 62

Green Bean & Lentil Salad 24

Griddled Cabbage Chop & Lentils 42

Griddled Sweet Potato & Quick Chimichurri 60

Griddled Vegetable Couscous 88

Halloumi Bake 186

Halloumi Saag 92

Halloumi Tikka Masala 120

Harissa-Baked Aubergine 148

Homemade Pasta 70

Hot Tabbouleh 150

Jollof Rice 68

Leek & Blue Cheese Tart 108

Leek & Mushroom Pot Pie 128

Leek & Spinach Lasagne 48

Lentil Soup 104

Messy Pea Lasagne 50

Milk Risotto 188

Mushroom Stroganoff 126

Nasi Goreng 30

Onion Biryani 36

Pea, Mint & Feta Salad 80

Pea Falafel 64

Peas, Pasta & Cream 46

Peperonata Sweet Potatoes 124

Pineapple Fried Rice 140

Pizza Frittata 168

Polenta Cornbread 52

Polenta-Crusted Aubergine 182

Portobello Kiev 146

Portobello Stilton Burger 66

Potato Focaccia 72

Potato & Leek Slice 82

Pulled BBQ Mushrooms 98

Puttanesca Bake 164

Roast Chickpea Gyros 44

Roasted Butternut Squash & Bulgur Wheat 26

Roasted Panzanella 34

Rotolo 176

Saag Aloo Samosas 196

Spicy Chilli Bean Sprouts 172

Spicy Patatas Bravas 20

Spinach Orecchiette 122

Sweet & Sour Peppers 32

Sweetcorn Bisque 28

Thai-Style Red Curry Noodles 118

Ultimate £1 Corn on the Cob 154

Vegan Lentil Chilli 38

Vegetable Cornish Pasty 40

Vegetable Hash 18

Vegetable Terrine 166

Welsh Rarebit & Tomato Pie 136

Yaki Soba 90

WELCOME

Welcome to my fifth cookbook, which is filled with quick, simple, economical and tasty meat-free recipes.

More and more people are trying to cut down on the amount of meat they consume. This totally makes sense – eating less meat can be healthier for you and much better for the environment – but a lifestyle change like this can be a bit daunting if you are unsure of how to incorporate meat-free meals into your weekly routine. This cookbook will provide you with plenty of ideas and the inspiration you need to get cooking without meat. Whether you're a meat eater, flexitarian, vegetarian or vegan, this book is packed with achievable and super-fast recipes that will get you cooking delicious food straight away.

I hope that this book becomes your companion and guide to cooking great-tasting, affordable meat-free food.

Miguel

MEAT-FREE CHALLENGE

The aim of this book is to help you slowly cut down on your meat intake and gently move you into the direction of a plant-based diet. My intention is to make it easy, stress-free and achievable to shift your mindset to a meat-free one and to get you confident cooking without meat. It can be difficult to change something so central to your daily life, but this book is the perfect start. It's simply not true that veg is bland, and it shouldn't be just a side dish. I'm here to show you how exciting and delicious it can be.

In addition to the health and environmental benefits, a meat-free diet has also been proven to be much cheaper. Once you cut meat out of the equation, the price of your weekly shop plummets and you can load up on even more fresh veg, grains, pulses, beans and lentils. You'll notice the vibrancy of the dishes, and you'll be getting loads more colour and freshness into your diet. This is cheerful food, food that will put a smile on your face and get you enthusiastic about cooking from scratch.

A lot of the recipes in this book are vegan-friendly and are a great stepping stone to incorporating more vegan food into your diet, but in a gentle and easy way. I have added notes and quick tips to many of the non-vegan recipes showing how to make simple substitutions to create fully vegan dishes – it's hacks like this that will soon become second nature to you as you embrace the meat-free life.

THE PRINCIPLES BEHIND ONE POUND MEALS

As with my previous books, I have taken my philosophies and principles of cooking on a budget and created a collection of meat-free recipes so you can jump straight in with confidence.

My One Pound Meals style of cooking has always been focused on simple techniques with plenty of easy shortcuts, using familiar ingredients that you're already comfortable buying and preparing. I want to help you save money by inspiring you to cook from scratch and give you confidence through the recipes I create. So I've written a meat-free cookbook for you, in my own relaxed style, with recipes that are inexpensive, straightforward and that feel familiar. These are the cornerstones of how I approach my One Pound Meals philosophy, and now I have applied them to meat-free dishes. I like my recipes to be friendly and welcoming; I want to encourage and nurture people to have a go.

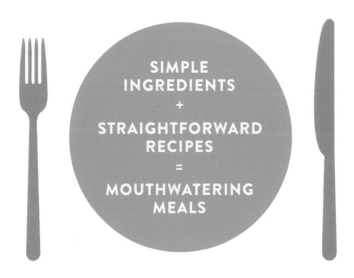

SIMPLE
INGREDIENTS
+
STRAIGHTFORWARD
RECIPES
=
MOUTHWATERING
MEALS

SIMPLE AND ECONOMICAL

This book is loaded with clever hacks and shortcuts to help you create delicious meals at home with minimal fuss, effort and expense. Just follow these recipes and you'll be adding more meals to your meat-free repertoire in no time at all.

Since my first book, the concept of One Pound Meals has evolved way beyond the £1 idea and is now its own style of cooking. This is the way I cook at home, using fewer ingredients and making recipes simpler. Mainly because it's easy, but also because it's delicious and economical. Just like in my previous books, these recipes still cost £1, but the £1 budget is now primarily my guiding force to eliminating superfluous ingredients, which in turn helps me reduce the number of steps in my recipes. It's the £1 budget that keeps my dishes simple and honest. There are no pre-made sauces with preservatives, E-numbers, and loads of salt. You'll be cooking from scratch, making tasty home-cooked food that will not only excite you but keep you in complete control over what you're eating.

ACHIEVABLE

To make my recipes achievable, a big part of my philosophy is to use ingredients that everyone is already familiar with. This is the key to getting people to give it a try at home. I haven't overly styled my food and I've kept it rustic in an effort to show you how achievable it is. This is weekday cooking, these are recipes that make your life easier with simple explanations and easy-to-follow steps. I like to think that when you see a Miguel Barclay recipe you'll think to yourself, 'I can totally see myself cooking that tonight.'

ALL RECIPES ARE FOR A SINGLE SERVING

MORE THAN ONE PERSON?

Simply multiply the ingredients to suit you.

FRENCH TOAST

One of my favourite brunches ever! Dipping bread into egg is such a simple concept, but the result is amazing. With a few berries and plenty of maple syrup, this makes a special weekend treat.

To make 1 portion

2 eggs

Pinch of cinnamon

2 slices of white bread

Small knob of butter (or splash of olive oil)

Sprinkle of icing sugar

A generous drizzle of maple syrup

A few blueberries

To cook

Crack the eggs into a dish big enough to lay a slice of bread into. Beat the eggs and add a pinch of cinnamon. Lay the bread in the dish to absorb the egg mixture for about 10 seconds on both sides, then repeat with the second slice.

Heat a frying pan over a medium heat and pan-fry the bread in some butter or olive oil for a few minutes on each side until the French toast is golden brown.

Transfer to a plate, lightly dust with icing sugar, drizzle with maple syrup and garnish with a few blueberries.

Make it vegan
To make this dish vegan, simply pan-fry the bread in vegan butter and cinnamon.

VEGETABLE HASH

A lot of the flavour in this dish comes from the charred and caramelised bits, so don't be scared to leave it in the pan a little longer.

To make 1 portion

½ courgette

½ carrot

½ potato

1 egg

Olive oil

Salt and pepper

To cook

Grate the courgette, carrot and potato onto a tea towel, sprinkle with salt and wring out as much water as possible by folding the edges of the tea towel together and twisting as hard as you can over the sink. Leave for a few minutes, then repeat to get the last bit of water out.

Heat a frying pan over a medium heat, add a splash of olive oil, then tip the hash into the pan and squash into a thin layer. Season, then leave it to fry gently without touching it for about 5 minutes until the bottom is golden brown. Flip using a fish slice and don't worry if it breaks, it's supposed to look messy. Give it another 5 minutes while you fry an egg in a separate pan and then serve.

SPICY PATATAS BRAVAS

Instead of the usual tomato-based sauce, here I've switched it up to a roasted red pepper sauce with a spicy kick.

To make 1 portion

Handful of small potatoes, skin on

200g roasted red peppers (from a 400g jar), plus half the oil

Squirt of sriracha

Pinch of dried oregano

1 spring onion, roughly chopped

Olive oil

Salt and pepper

To cook

Cook the potatoes in a pan of salted boiling water for about 15 minutes until soft. Drain and let them steam for a bit to dry out.

Transfer the potatoes to a frying pan and squash each one slightly with the back of a fork to break the skins and expose the fluffy middle. Season and fry the potatoes in a generous glug of olive oil for about 20 minutes until crispy all over.

Meanwhile, to make the sauce, grab a blender and add the roasted red peppers, along with the oil from the jar, the sriracha, oregano and a pinch of salt. Blend and then pour into the pan with the potatoes. Simmer for a couple of minutes to warm the sauce, then add the chopped spring onion and some cracked black pepper, and serve.

BLACK BEAN & CHILLI ENCHILADAS

I love enchiladas, they are one of my go-to comfort foods. Rice and beans together in a convenient wrap is such a good idea. And then finished off with some melted cheese on top . . . They tick every box.

To make 1 portion

½ mug of basmati rice

1 mug of water for the rice, plus 25ml for the tortillas

½ red onion, sliced

1 tsp cumin seeds

100g black beans (from a 400g tin), drained

½ red chilli, sliced

Small handful of chopped coriander

40g plain flour

Splash of tomato passata

Small handful of grated Cheddar cheese

Olive oil

Salt and pepper

To cook

Start by putting the rice and the mug of water in a saucepan and simmering over a medium heat with the lid on for about 7 minutes until all the water has been absorbed and the rice is cooked. Remove from the heat and fluff with a fork.

Meanwhile, pan-fry the onion in a splash of olive oil over a medium heat for a few minutes before adding the cumin seeds. Continue frying for a minute then add the black beans and sliced chilli. Season with salt and pepper and continue to fry for a few more minutes before removing from the heat and adding the chopped coriander.

Make the tortillas by mixing the flour with the 25ml of water and a pinch of salt in a bowl. Knead on a floured worktop until smooth, then cut into 2 balls. Using a rolling pin, roll each ball into a circle approximately 15cm in diameter. Heat a dry frying pan over a high heat, place the tortillas, one at a time, in the pan and cook for about 5 seconds on each side.

Preheat the grill to high. Spoon half the rice and half the beans down the centre of each tortilla, then roll up and place in an ovenproof dish. Top with a splash of tomato passata, add a pinch each of salt and pepper and then sprinkle over the grated Cheddar.

Cook for about 7 minutes under the grill until the cheese is melted, then serve.

Make it vegan
To make this dish vegan, substitute the cheese with a plant-based cheese.

GREEN BEAN & LENTIL SALAD

A great shortcut when you have little time is to use pre-cooked lentils. They are so versatile and take on flavours really well. Here we are mixing hot and cold ingredients to create a salad with a zingy Dijon-based dressing.

To make 1 portion

1 small potato, cut into slices

1 egg

Small handful of green beans

4 tbsp olive oil

1 tbsp red wine vinegar

1 tsp Dijon mustard

100g cooked green lentils (from a 400g tin), drained

Salt and pepper

To cook

Start by boiling the potato slices in a pan of salted water. After a couple of minutes, add the egg and boil for exactly 6½ minutes. Put the egg into a bowl of cold water to stop the cooking process and throw the beans into the boiling water. After a couple of minutes, when the beans and potato slices are cooked, drain and set to one side.

To make the dressing, mix the olive oil with the red wine vinegar and Dijon mustard, then season with a pinch each of salt and pepper.

Mix the lentils with the green beans and potato slices. Peel the egg, cut it in half and add it to the salad, then dress with the Dijon dressing.

Make it vegan
To make this dish vegan, substitute the egg with tofu or simply leave it out altogether.

ROASTED BUTTERNUT SQUASH & BULGUR WHEAT

One butternut squash goes far, so it's important to have a few easy recipes up your sleeve to keep it exciting on day 3, 4 or even 5. This is a dish I love to cook – I really like the combination of bulgur wheat, parsley and salty feta with the slightly sweet squash.

To make 1 portion

A few slices of butternut squash (skin on)

Handful of bulgur wheat

Handful of chopped parsley

Small handful of crumbled feta

Olive oil

Salt and pepper

To cook

Preheat your oven to 190°C/gas mark 5.

Put the butternut squash in a roasting tray, drizzle with olive oil and season with a pinch each of salt and pepper, then roast in the oven for about 30 minutes until soft and cooked through.

Meanwhile, cook the bulgur wheat in a saucepan of salted boiling water for about 10 minutes until cooked, then drain. Mix the drained bulgur wheat in a bowl with the chopped parsley, top with the crumbled feta and serve with the roasted butternut squash.

SWEETCORN BISQUE

This isn't really a bisque but I couldn't think what to call it . . . It's a combination of slightly charred peppers with a piquant tomato sauce sweetened with a splash of cream. Delicious.

To make 1 portion

Handful of mini sweetcorn, cut in half lengthways

½ red onion, very thinly sliced

1 garlic clove, sliced

200g chopped tomatoes (from a 400g tin)

½ tsp hot paprika

Splash of single cream

Olive oil

Salt and pepper

To cook

Start by pan-frying the sweetcorn in a splash of olive oil over a medium heat for about 5 minutes until slightly charred. Then remove from the pan and set to one side.

Next, add the onions and garlic, season then pan-fry for about 5 minutes until the garlic starts to colour. At this point, add the chopped tomatoes, season and add half a teaspoon of paprika. Simmer for about 7 minutes before adding a splash of cream, topping with the sweetcorn and serving with a drizzle of olive oil.

Make it vegan

To make this dish vegan, substitute the splash of cream with a plant-based cream.

NASI GORENG

Toasted sesame oil is the key to this dish. Have a bottle of it in your kitchen and you'll be eating Asian food that tastes so authentic that you'll be amazed you made it in your own home.

To make 1 portion

½ mug of brown rice

1 mug of water

Wedge of Savoy cabbage, finely shredded

Sesame oil

½ carrot, cut into matchsticks

1 garlic clove, crushed

Soy sauce

1 egg

Squirt of sriracha

To cook

Put the rice and water in a saucepan and cook over a medium heat with the lid on for about 15 minutes, until all the water has been absorbed and the rice is cooked. Remove the lid and allow to cool.

Pan-fry the cabbage in a splash of sesame oil over a medium-high heat for a few minutes, then add the carrot. Fry for a few more minutes then add the cooled rice, crushed garlic, a splash of soy sauce and a splash more sesame oil. Fry for another 3 minutes and transfer to a plate or bowl.

Fry the egg in the pan then place it on top of the rice and finish with a squirt of sriracha.

SWEET & SOUR PEPPERS

It's amazing how much this quick cheat's version of a sweet and sour actually tastes like the real thing. So why not try swapping your Friday-night takeaway for this £1 version.

To make 1 portion

½ mug of basmati rice

1 mug of water

2 tbsp plain flour

¼ red pepper, roughly diced

¼ yellow pepper, roughly diced

¼ green pepper, roughly diced

½ onion, roughly diced

Splash of sesame oil

1 tsp demerara sugar

Big squirt of tomato ketchup

Splash of rice wine vinegar

A few pineapple slices from a tin, plus some of the juice

Salt and pepper

To cook

First put the rice and water into a saucepan and simmer over a medium heat with the lid on for about 7 minutes until all the water has been absorbed and the rice is cooked.

While the rice is cooking, season the flour and dust the peppers and onions, then pan-fry in a splash of sesame oil over a medium heat for about 5 minutes. At this point add the sugar, ketchup and vinegar and continue to fry for a further minute before adding the pineapple and some of the juice. Simmer for another minute to thicken the sauce slightly, season to taste and serve with the rice.

ROASTED PANZANELLA

Roasting the ingredients of a traditional panzanella salad transforms it into a delicious main course meal with a much more intense flavour.

To make 1 portion

Handful of cherry tomatoes

½ red onion, quartered

2 pinches of dried oregano

5 slices of ciabatta

Small handful of rocket

Drizzle of balsamic glaze

Olive oil

Salt and pepper

To cook

Preheat your oven to 190°C/gas mark 5.

Put the cherry tomatoes and onion quarters in a roasting tray and drizzle with olive oil. Add a pinch of the oregano and a pinch each of salt and pepper, then roast in the oven for about 15 minutes.

Meanwhile, drizzle the ciabatta slices with olive oil and sprinkle over the remaining oregano. Toast on a hot griddle pan over a medium heat on both sides until nicely charred (you could pan-fry or oven-bake the ciabatta if you prefer).

Assemble the panzanella by placing the roasted vegetables on the toasted ciabatta slices, along with the rocket, and drizzle with olive oil and balsamic glaze.

ONION BIRYANI

Here, I slowly caramelise red onions to create a gorgeous sticky, sweet base to replace the meat in a typical biryani. Packed with flavour, this dish is a winner.

To make 1 portion

2 red onions, thinly sliced

½ tsp curry powder

½ vegetable stock cube

¼ mug of basmati rice

½ mug of water

Pinch of turmeric

Pinch of desiccated coconut

Olive oil

Salt and pepper

To cook

Preheat your oven to 190°C/gas mark 5.

Slowly pan-fry the onions in a splash of olive oil over a low-medium heat with a pinch of salt. After about 15 minutes, when the onions have started to caramelise, add the curry powder and crumble in the stock cube. Fry for a few more minutes, then transfer to an ovenproof dish. Top with the rice, pour over the water and add the turmeric. Season then cover the dish tightly with a sheet of foil and bake in the oven for about 30 minutes until all the water has been absorbed by the rice and the rice is cooked. Sprinkle with the desiccated coconut and serve.

VEGAN LENTIL CHILLI

Chilli is a great idea for a social occasion. One big pot in the middle of the table makes for a casual and relaxed catch-up with friends and family.

To make 1 portion

½ red onion, sliced

1 garlic clove, sliced

Handful of Puy lentils

1 tsp ground cumin

200g chopped tomatoes (from a 400g tin)

1 mug of water for the chilli, plus 1 mug for the rice

1 vegetable stock cube

100g kidney beans (from a 400g tin), drained

½ mug of basmati rice

Small handful of chopped coriander

Olive oil

Salt and pepper

To cook

Grab a saucepan and fry the onion and garlic in a splash of olive oil over a medium heat. After about 5 minutes, just as the garlic is starting to brown, add the Puy lentils, a teaspoon of cumin, the chopped tomatoes, a mug of water and the stock cube. Season then simmer for about 10–15 minutes until the lentils are cooked and the sauce has reduced to a thicker consistency. About 5 minutes before the end of the cooking time, add the drained kidney beans.

Meanwhile, put the rice and a mug of water into a saucepan and cook over a medium heat with the lid on for about 7 minutes until all the water has been absorbed and the rice is cooked. Fluff with a fork and stir in some chopped coriander, then serve with the chilli.

VEGETABLE CORNISH PASTY

The main seasoning in a Cornish pasty is pepper, so don't be shy. Give yours a bit of a peppery kick. Another top tip is to chop your potatoes small so they won't need any pre-cooking: it all happens inside the pastry.

To make 1 portion

¼ medium potato, diced

¼ carrot, diced

¼ onion, diced

1 mushroom, grated

Small handful of frozen peas

¼ vegetable stock cube

20cm diameter circle of shortcrust pastry

1 egg, beaten

Salt and pepper

To cook

Preheat your oven to 190°C/gas mark 5 and line a baking tray with greaseproof paper.

Mix the diced potato, carrot and onion in a bowl with the grated mushroom and frozen peas. Crumble in the stock cube, mix again and season with salt and plenty of pepper.

Put the pastry circle on the lined baking tray then place the vegetable mixture in the middle of the pastry circle. Fold the pastry in half and fold the edges over each other to create the classic pasty shape. Alternatively, just squash the edges together using the back of a fork. Brush the pasty with beaten egg then bake in the oven for about 40 minutes until golden brown.

Make it vegan

Brush the pasty with olive oil and use vegan shortcrust pastry.

GRIDDLED CABBAGE CHOP & LENTILS

Griddled cabbage is a great meat substitute. The caramelisation of the char marks gives the cabbage a nice depth of flavour that mimics the effect of barbecuing or pan-frying meat. Here, I've paired it with a lentil salad topped with a crème fraîche dressing.

To make 1 portion

2 wedges of white cabbage

200g green lentils (from a 400g tin), drained

¼ vegetable stock cube

Small handful of chopped parsley

1 tbsp crème fraîche

Pinch of dried oregano

Olive oil

Salt and pepper

To cook

Preheat your griddle pan (or a frying pan) over a medium-high heat.

Drizzle the cabbage 'chops' with olive oil and season with a pinch each of salt and pepper, then cook for about 5 minutes on each side in the hot pan, until cooked through (with nice char lines, if you're using a griddle).

Meanwhile, put the drained lentils in a bowl, crumble in the stock cube, add a pinch each of salt and pepper and a splash of olive oil and mix. Add the chopped parsley and mix again. Season the crème fraîche with a pinch each of salt and pepper and add the oregano. Serve the cabbage chop with the lentils and drizzle with the crème fraîche.

Make it vegan
Swap the crème fraîche for dairy-free cream, or leave it out.

ROAST CHICKPEA GYROS

Oven-roasting chickpeas with olive oil, cumin and paprika creates an intensely flavoured filling for a gyro. The chickpeas have a slight crunch and are perfect for wrapping in a warm flatbread with loads of salad and a creamy sauce.

To make 1 portion

200g chickpeas (from a 400g tin), drained

1 tsp ground cumin

1 tsp smoked paprika

40g plain flour, plus extra for dusting

25ml cold water

2 tbsp crème fraîche

Pinch of dried oregano

A few lettuce leaves

A few cherry tomatoes, chopped

A few slices of red onion

Olive oil

Salt and pepper

To cook

Preheat your oven to 190°C/gas mark 5.

Put the chickpeas in an ovenproof dish with a glug of olive oil, the cumin, paprika and a pinch each of salt and pepper. Roast in the oven for about 20 minutes until golden brown.

Meanwhile, to make the flatbread, mix the flour and water in a bowl with a pinch of salt to form a dough. Dust the worktop with a little flour, then knead the dough for a minute until smooth. Roll into a circle about 20cm in diameter.

Heat a dry frying pan or griddle over a high heat, add the flatbread and cook for a minute on each side until nicely toasted.

Make the sauce by mixing the crème fraîche in a bowl with a pinch each of salt and pepper and the oregano, then assemble the gyro by stuffing the flatbread with lettuce, tomato, onion, sauce and roasted chickpeas, then folding it in half.

Make it vegan
Swap the crème fraîche for vegan cream or vegan yogurt.

PEAS, PASTA & CREAM *+ pesto!*

This is such a simple dish but it looks quite cool and is packed with so much flavour from the pepper and Parmesan in the sauce. It doesn't really matter which pasta you use here, I only used mafalda corta because it had been sitting in my kitchen for ages and I wanted to use it up.

To make 1 portion

Handful of pasta

Handful of frozen peas

2 spring onions, roughly chopped

150ml single cream

Handful of grated Parmesan cheese, plus extra to serve

Olive oil

Salt and pepper

To cook

Cook the pasta in a pan of salted boiling water as per the instructions on the packet, adding the peas a few minutes before the end. Then drain, reserving some of the pasta cooking water for the sauce.

While the pasta is cooking, pan-fry the spring onions in a splash of olive oil over a medium heat for a few minutes until soft, then add the cream and simmer for 1 minute. Remove from the heat, stir in the Parmesan and season with salt and pepper. Add the pasta and the peas, along with a few tablespoons of the pasta water, and mix together. Serve with an extra sprinkle of Parmesan and a drizzle of olive oil.

LEEK & SPINACH LASAGNE

This vegetarian lasagne with a bechamel sauce base is packed with flavour. It has only one layer, which is a neat little trick to save time.

To make 1 portion

1 leek, sliced

200g frozen spinach, defrosted

2 tsp butter

2 tsp plain flour

200ml milk

Handful of grated Cheddar cheese

2 dried lasagne sheets

Olive oil

Salt and pepper

To cook

Preheat your oven to 190°C/gas mark 5.

Pan-fry the sliced leek in a splash of olive oil over a medium heat for a few minutes until soft. Season, then add the defrosted spinach and continue to fry for a few more minutes before removing from the heat.

Grab a saucepan and melt the butter over a medium heat. Add the flour and continue to cook for 2 minutes, stirring continuously, then add the milk in small quantities while stirring all the time. When the sauce is made and all the lumps have dissolved, remove from the heat and add the grated Cheddar, reserving a small amount for later.

Transfer the leeks to an ovenproof dish and pour over half the bechamel sauce (or keep the leeks in the pan if the pan is oven proof). Lay the lasagne sheets on top in a cross pattern and then spoon the remaining bechamel sauce on top of the lasagne sheets. Sprinkle with the remaining cheese and bake in the oven for about 30 minutes until bubbling and golden brown at the edges.

Make it vegan

To make this dish vegan, substitute the butter, milk and cheese with vegan/plant-based alternatives.

MESSY PEA LASAGNE

This is a super-speedy meal made from just three ingredients; it can be cobbled together at a moment's notice. The goat's cheese gives it a lovely depth of flavour and the crispy lasagne sheet adds texture to this very simple dish.

To make 1 portion

Handful of frozen peas

Handful of crumbled goat's cheese

1 dried lasagne sheet

Olive oil

Salt and pepper

To cook

Preheat the grill to high.

Put the frozen peas into a pan of boiling water, and as soon as the water starts to boil again, remove from the heat and drain. Transfer to an ovenproof dish, season with salt and pepper, then scatter over half the crumbled goat's cheese.

Soften the lasagne sheet in a bowl of boiling water for a few minutes. Lay the lasagne sheet on top of the peas and goat's cheese, folding it in half, then add the remaining goat's cheese. Season with another pinch each of salt and pepper, then drizzle with olive oil.

Cook under the grill for about 5 minutes until the lasagne sheet has turned golden brown at the edges, then serve.

POLENTA CORNBREAD

Cornbread is a filling bread you can make easily at home, without all the hassle of actually baking with yeast. I like to drizzle my cornbread with maple syrup at the end for a nice sweet glaze.

To make 1 cornbread

100g polenta

1 egg

50g self-raising flour

75g milk

Pinch of chilli flakes

Handful of tinned sweetcorn

1 tbsp maple syrup

Olive oil

Salt and pepper

To cook

Preheat the oven to 190°C/gas mark 5.

Mix the polenta, egg, flour, milk, chilli flakes and sweetcorn in a bowl, season with salt and pepper, then spoon the mixture into an oiled round ovenproof dish roughly 15cm in diameter.

Bake for about 30 minutes until golden brown, then remove from the oven and drizzle with maple syrup before serving.

CANNELLINI BEANS WITH LEEK & TOMATOES

This simple, humble bean stew is perfect for eating on a budget. The splash of red wine vinegar gives it a great little kick. If you're not confident with balancing flavours with vinegar, then this is the dish to get you started: just give it a taste before and after and you'll see the difference it makes.

To make 1 portion

¼ leek, roughly chopped

1 garlic clove, sliced

Handful of cherry tomatoes

200g cannellini beans (from a 400g tin), drained

Pinch of dried oregano

½ vegetable stock cube

Small splash of red wine vinegar

Olive oil

Salt and pepper

To cook

Pan-fry the leek, garlic and tomatoes in a generous glug of olive oil over a medium heat, with a pinch each of salt and pepper, for about 5 minutes. When the garlic starts to brown, add the beans and oregano, and crumble in the stock cube. Fry for another couple of minutes, then add the splash of red wine vinegar and a splash of water. Simmer for a few minutes, then serve, drizzled with a generous glug of olive oil.

CACIO E PEPE

A traditional cacio e pepe uses a pasta called bucatini, but really any pasta will do. I spent ages trying to find bucatini and it was a complete nightmare. Spaghetti works just as well and I'm sure no one will notice.

To make 1 portion

125g spaghetti

3 tbsp butter

Small handful of grated Parmesan cheese

Salt and pepper

To cook

Cook the pasta in a pan of boiling salted water as per the instructions on the packet, then drain, reserving some of the pasta cooking water.

Heat the butter in a pan over a medium heat until it starts bubbling, then add a few tablespoons of the pasta water while stirring continuously. After a couple of minutes remove from the heat and add the grated Parmesan and loads of black pepper, stirring for a few minutes until the sauce thickens a little. Add the cooked pasta, mix well, then serve.

GRIDDLED SWEET POTATO & QUICK CHIMICHURRI

This is a really simple way to prepare your sweet potatoes: just slice them and whack them on a griddle pan. The herby sauce is a cheat's version of real chimichurri. It's much easier to make and goes perfectly with the sweet potato.

To make 1 portion

½ sweet potato, cut into long, 1cm-thick slices

1 tbsp red wine vinegar

¼ red onion, finely diced

1 garlic clove, crushed

Handful of chopped parsley

Handful of watercress

Olive oil

Salt and pepper

To cook

Preheat a griddle pan or frying pan.

Drizzle the sweet potato slices with olive oil and season with salt. Place them on the hot griddle or frying pan and cook for about 20 minutes until cooked through, turning them after 10 minutes.

Meanwhile, to make the sauce, mix 8 tablespoons of olive oil with the red wine vinegar, diced onion, crushed garlic and chopped parsley in a bowl.

Serve the griddled sweet potato slices on a bed of watercress topped with the herby sauce and some cracked black pepper.

GREEN BEAN & LENTIL CURRY

Lentils are a delicious way to bulk out a meal, and they take on other flavours really well. This fantastic lentil-based curry uses pre-cooked lentils, which means it takes no time at all to make.

To make 1 portion

½ onion, sliced

1 garlic clove, sliced

Small handful of green beans

1 tsp curry powder

200g green lentils (from a 400g tin), drained

½ vegetable stock cube

Splash of cream

Olive oil

Salt and pepper

To cook

Pan-fry the sliced onion, garlic and green beans in a splash of olive oil over a medium heat for a few minutes until the garlic starts to brown, then add the curry powder and the lentils. Fry for another minute, then add a big splash of water, crumble in the stock cube and simmer for a few minutes until the beans are cooked and the sauce thickens.

Season to taste with salt and pepper and serve with a splash of cream.

Make it vegan
To make this dish vegan, swap the splash of cream for a plant-based cream.

PEA FALAFEL

Frozen spinach is great for binding these falafels together without needing to use egg, and is the key to making these vegan bites so tasty.

To make 1 portion

Handful of frozen peas

3 blocks of frozen spinach (about 50g)

2 tbsp chickpea flour (gram flour)

1 tsp ground cumin

A few lettuce leaves

A few slices of red onion

A few slices of radish

Olive oil

Salt and pepper

To cook

Let the peas and spinach sit at room temperature to defrost (or use a microwave), then blitz in a food processor with the chickpea flour, cumin and a pinch each of salt and pepper.

Heat a splash of olive oil in a frying pan over a medium heat. Using a tablespoon, add dollops of the falafel mixture to the frying pan (the mixture should make about 6 falafels) and cook, turning them over after a couple of minutes, until nicely browned.

Serve the falafels on lettuce 'boats', with slices of onion and radish.

PORTOBELLO STILTON BURGER

This is so simple to make. Just crumble some Stilton onto a mushroom, bake it, and there you have it: my quick and easy veggie burger. The potatoes become sort of like nuggets when they're cooked and are a perfect accompaniment.

To make 1 portion

A few small potatoes, skin on

1 portobello mushroom

Small handful of Stilton

1 bread bun, toasted

A few lettuce leaves

Squeeze of tomato ketchup

Olive oil

Salt

To cook

Preheat your oven to 190°C/gas mark 5.

Cook the potatoes in a pan of salted boiling water for about 15 minutes until soft. Drain and let them steam for a bit to dry out.

Transfer the potatoes to an ovenproof dish and squash each one slightly with the back of a fork to break the skin and expose the fluffy middle. Pour over a generous glug of olive oil, add a pinch of salt and roast for about 40 minutes until crispy.

When the potatoes have about 15 minutes of cooking time left, brush the outside of the mushroom with olive oil, turn it upside down and crumble the Stilton into it. Place on a baking tray and cook for about 15 minutes in the oven until the mushroom is cooked and the cheese has totally melted.

Serve the mushroom burger in a toasted bun with a few lettuce leaves alongside the crispy potatoes and a ketchup dip.

JOLLOF RICE

This is a rich and spicy rice dish with stewed onions, garlic, tomatoes and plenty of dried chilli flakes, but with the cooling addition of sliced banana at the end.

To make 1 portion

1 tbsp tomato purée

½ onion, roughly diced

1 garlic clove, sliced

½ red pepper, roughly diced

Generous pinch of chilli flakes

200g chopped tomatoes (from a 400g tin)

½ mug of rice

1 mug of water

½ vegetable stock cube

½ banana, sliced

Olive oil

Salt and pepper

To cook

Start by grabbing a high-sided pan and pan-frying the tomato purée, onion, garlic and red pepper in a splash of oil over a medium heat for about 5 minutes. Then add the chilli flakes, chopped tomatoes, rice, water and stock cube. Season and simmer for about 10 minutes until the rice is cooked (adding more water if required). Finally, add the chopped banana, season to taste and serve.

HOMEMADE PASTA

You can serve this with a lovely tomato ragu but I want to show you just how simple it can be when you make the pasta the star of the show.

To make 1 portion

90g tipo '00' flour

25g semolina flour

1 large egg

1 egg yolk

2 tbsp butter

A few sage leaves

Handful of grated Parmesan cheese

Olive oil

Salt and pepper

To cook

Mix together both the flours, the egg and egg yolk in a bowl and then tip the mixture out on a floured worktop. Knead for about 5 minutes until smooth. Wrap in cling film and refrigerate for around an hour.

Bring a pan of salted water to the boil.

Cut the dough ball into quarters to make it easier to handle and using a rolling pin roll the dough as thin as you can (about 1mm or 2mm thick). Keep dusting with semolina flour to stop it sticking. Cut each piece of dough into strips about 5cm wide. Cook the pasta in the boiling salted water for a few minutes, then drain.

Melt the butter in a pan over a medium heat and when it starts bubbling add the sage leaves and fry for a minute in the butter.

Add the cooked pasta to the pan with the butter and sage, remove from the heat, add the Parmesan and then serve with a splash of olive oil and plenty of cracked black pepper.

POTATO FOCACCIA

Cutting potatoes in a spiral increases the surface area when cooking, and makes them twice as crispy. But if you want a quicker method, just slice the potatoes instead, and scatter over some chopped rosemary.

To make 1 portion

100g strong flour

3.5g dried yeast

100ml warm water

4 small potatoes

4 rosemary sprigs

Olive oil

Salt and pepper

To cook

Grease a 20 x 10cm oven tray with oil. Put the flour, yeast and water in a bowl along with a pinch of salt, and mix to form a dough. Tip the dough into the greased oven tray, drizzle the dough with olive oil, cover with cling film and leave in a warm place for 1 hour.

Preheat your oven to 190°C/gas mark 5.

Grab a potato and skewer it from end to end with a chopstick. Cut into the potato in a spiral formation, from one end to the other (the chopstick will prevent you cutting all the way through the potato), then remove the chopstick and insert a sprig of rosemary in its place, stretching out the potato spiral along the sprig to open it up.

Repeat with the remaining potatoes and rosemary sprigs then drizzle them with olive oil and season with salt and pepper. Once the dough has risen, remove the cling film, squash the skewered, spiral potatoes into the dough and bake in the oven for about 30 minutes until golden brown.

FETA GOUJONS

I came up with this dish while I was experimenting with making feta goujons and chips. The goujons just worked better as a posh salad with roasted cherry tomatoes – perfect for a summer's day.

To make 1 portion

100g feta, cut into slices

1 tbsp plain flour

1 egg, beaten

Small handful of breadcrumbs (grated stale bread)

Small handful of cherry tomatoes

Handful of rocket

Olive oil

Salt and pepper

To cook

Preheat your oven to 190°C/gas mark 5.

Dust the feta slices with plain flour, dip them in the beaten egg and then roll them in the breadcrumbs. Place on a lined baking tray and cook in the oven for about 25 minutes until golden brown.

Place the tomatoes in an ovenproof dish, add a splash of olive oil and a pinch each of salt and pepper, then cook in the oven for about 15 minutes until soft and gooey.

When the feta goujons and tomatoes are cooked, serve them hot on a handful of rocket.

Make it vegan
To make this dish vegan, substitute the feta for a plant-based Greek-style cheese. Substitute the egg by brushing the cheese with a little oil before dipping in the breadcrumbs (no need to dust with flour).

AUBERGINE MILANESE

Here's my meat-free twist on a classic Italian dish. I really love the contrasting texture of the crispy seasoned breadcrumbs and the buttery soft aubergine.

To make 1 portion

1 tbsp plain flour

1 egg

Handful of breadcrumbs (grated stale bread)

1cm-thick slice of aubergine

100g spaghetti

¼ onion, diced

1 garlic clove, sliced

200g chopped tomatoes (from a 400g tin)

Olive oil

Salt and pepper

To cook

Bring a saucepan of salted water to the boil.

Grab three shallow bowls. Put the flour in one, crack the egg into another and beat it, and put the breadcrumbs in the third. Season the breadcrumbs with salt and pepper. Coat the aubergine slice in flour, then the egg, then the breadcrumbs.

Pan-fry the aubergine in a splash of olive oil over a medium heat for about 7 minutes on each side until golden brown and cooked through.

While the aubergine is in the pan, add the spaghetti to the boiling water and cook until al dente.

In a separate pan, fry the onion and garlic in a splash of olive oil over a medium heat for a few minutes. Once the onions are cooked and just

as the garlic starts to brown, add the chopped tomatoes, season with salt and pepper and simmer for about 10 minutes until the tomatoes have broken down to make a nice sauce. Using tongs, transfer the cooked pasta from the saucepan to the frying pan with the pasta sauce and stir. Serve with the breaded, fried aubergine.

Make it vegan

Substitute the egg for aquafaba (whipped-up liquid from a tin of chickpeas) and make sure you use 100 per cent durum wheat pasta made without egg.

CAULIFLOWER TACOS

These tasty meat-free tacos are made with cauliflower florets pan-fried with cumin seeds and a zingy lime-dressed salad. By making your own tortillas, this dish comes in at well under £1.

To make I portion

¼ cauliflower

Pinch of cumin seeds

Squirt of sriracha

2 tbsp mayonnaise

40g plain flour

25ml cold water

Handful of thinly sliced red cabbage

½ red onion, thinly sliced

Small handful of chopped coriander

½ lime

Olive oil

Salt and pepper

To cook

Cut the cauliflower into florets, then pan-fry them in a splash of olive oil and a pinch each of salt and pepper over a medium heat for a few minutes, until the cauliflower starts to colour. Add the cumin seeds and fry for a few more minutes until the cauliflower is tender. Remove from the heat and set to one side.

Combine the sriracha and mayo in a small bowl.

To make the tacos, put the flour and water in a bowl with a pinch of salt and mix to create a dough. Knead on a work surface until the dough is smooth, then separate it into three pieces and roll each piece into a ball. Roll each ball into a circle about 10cm in diameter.

Heat a frying pan over a high heat. Toast the tacos in the hot pan one at a time for a few minutes on each side until lightly toasted.

To make the salad, mix the cabbage and onion in a bowl, add the coriander and squeeze over the juice from the half lime. Add a splash of olive oil and season with salt and pepper, then let it rest for about 10 minutes to soften the onion in the lime juice.

Assemble the tacos, placing a few florets on a bed of the salad, and top with the sriracha mayo.

Make it vegan
Leave out the mayo, or replace it with dairy-free yogurt.

PEA, MINT & FETA SALAD

This recipe always makes an appearance at my barbecues. It is just so easy, and it's more of an interesting and substantial dish than a traditional salad made with lettuce and tomato.

To make 1 portion

Big handful of frozen peas

Small handful of frozen broad beans

Handful of chopped mint

1 red chilli, sliced

Small handful of crumbled feta

Olive oil

Salt and pepper

To make

Put the peas and broad beans in a colander and run hot water from the tap over them until they have defrosted, then shell the broad beans. Tip into a bowl, dress with a splash of olive oil and season with a pinch each of salt and pepper, then add the mint, chilli and feta and mix to combine.

POTATO & LEEK SLICE

This is my version of the famous Greggs cheese and onion slice and is packed with so much flavour. Best eaten in slices.

To make 1 portion

1 potato, diced

1 leek, sliced

Small handful of grated Cheddar cheese

20 x 20cm sheet of puff pastry

1 egg, beaten

Olive oil

Salt and pepper

To cook

Season and pan-fry the diced potato in a splash of olive oil over a medium heat for about 10 minutes until soft, then add the sliced leek and continue to pan-fry for another 5 minutes. Transfer to a bowl, add the Cheddar and mix everything together, crushing the potatoes slightly.

Line a rectangular dish approximately 10 x 5cm with cling film. Transfer the filling to the dish and squash it down with the back of a spoon. Refrigerate for about 1 hour until it sets into a block shape.

Preheat your oven to 190°C/gas mark 5.

Remove the block of filling from the dish and wrap it in the sheet of puff pastry. Place on a lined baking tray, brush with beaten egg and bake in the oven for about 30 minutes until golden brown, then serve.

CHINESE-STYLE OYSTER MUSHROOMS

You can make this dish with any type of mushroom, or any veg really, but I find oyster mushrooms have a wonderfully meaty texture that make this a satisfying and substantial alternative to a Friday night Chinese takeaway.

To make 1 portion

½ mug of basmati rice

1 mug of water

Handful of oyster mushrooms

Splash of sesame oil

1 garlic clove, sliced

Squeeze of golden syrup or honey

Squeeze of sriracha

Soy sauce

Pinch of sesame seeds

½ spring onion, sliced

To cook

Put the rice and water in a saucepan and cook over a medium heat with the lid on for about 7 minutes, until all the water has been absorbed and the rice is cooked.

Meanwhile, pan-fry the oyster mushrooms in a splash of sesame oil over a medium heat for a few minutes, then add the garlic and fry for a few more minutes until the garlic starts to brown. Add the golden syrup and sriracha and simmer for a few minutes until the sauce starts to thicken, then stir in a splash of soy sauce.

Serve the mushrooms on a bed of basmati rice and sprinkle with the sesame seeds and spring onion.

Make it vegan
Using golden syrup rather than honey makes this dish vegan.

CAULIFLOWER 3 WAYS

I remember one summer when the price of a cauliflower dropped to under 50p: that would feed a family of four for £1! At any time of year, however, it's a great-value vegetable. The key to turning it into a complete dish is to treat some of the cauliflower like potatoes, to act as 'carbs', pick some nice-looking florets and turn them into the 'meat', and use the leaves (don't throw them away – they taste amazing!) to form the 'veg' element.

To make 1 portion

½ cauliflower

Olive oil

Salt and pepper

To cook

Bring a pan of salted water to the boil.

Separate the leaves from the cauliflower and set them aside, and pick off a few nice-looking florets. Boil the rest of the cauliflower in the pan of salted water for about 10 minutes, until it is soft enough to mash.

While the cauliflower is cooking, pan-fry the florets in a glug of olive oil over a medium heat – seasoning them with a pinch each of salt and pepper – for about 10 minutes until nicely charred and golden brown. Remove from the pan, set to one side, then pan-fry the leaves (adding more oil to the pan if needed) over a medium heat with some more salt and pepper for a few minutes until the thick central ribs have softened.

Drain the boiled cauliflower, mash it with a splash of olive oil and a pinch each of salt and pepper, then serve with the pan-fried florets and the leaves.

GRIDDLED VEGETABLE COUSCOUS

This is a great recipe for when you have loads of leftover veg. Just chuck them on a hot griddle pan until they have char marks. The couscous bulks out a few vegetables to create a delicious plate of food, and the feta is a lovely, decadent topping.

To make 1 portion

A few long 5mm-thick slices of courgette

A few 5mm-thick slices of red pepper

A few 5mm-thick slices of red onion

Pinch of dried oregano

¼ vegetable stock cube

¼ mug of boiling water

¼ mug of couscous

Small handful of crumbled feta

Olive oil

Salt and pepper

To cook

Preheat your griddle pan (or a frying pan) over a medium-high heat.

Coat the vegetables in a splash of olive oil and sprinkle with a pinch each of salt and pepper and the oregano. Cook them on the hot pan for a couple of minutes on each side until nicely charred and tender.

Dissolve the stock cube in the boiling water, then add the stock to the mug of couscous. Let it rest for about 5 minutes, then fluff the couscous with a fork and mix with the griddled veg. Top with the crumbled feta and serve.

Make it vegan
Leave out the feta to make this dish vegan-friendly.

YAKI SOBA

This is my £1 version of the famous Wagamama Yaki Soba noodles. The distinctive flavour comes from using leeks instead of onion and adding a pinch of curry powder. And it totally works!

To make 1 portion

¼ leek, sliced

Splash of sesame oil

Pinch of curry powder

¼ green pepper, sliced

A few mushrooms, sliced

Small handful of bean sprouts

100g udon noodles

1 egg

Pinch of sesame seeds

A few slices of carrot, cut into matchsticks

Salt and pepper

To cook

Pan-fry the leeks in a splash of sesame oil and a pinch of curry powder over a high heat. After a couple of minutes, once the leeks have softened, add the peppers, mushrooms and bean sprouts and continue to pan-fry for a few more minutes.

Cook the noodles as per the instructions on the packet then drain and add to the pan.

Move everything to the side of the pan and crack an egg into the empty side. Once the egg is about 80 per cent cooked, scramble with a wooden spoon and mix everything together. Season to taste and serve with a sprinkle of sesame seeds and some chopped carrot.

HALLOUMI SAAG

Halloumi just got even better! Pan-frying it in curry powder gives it a beautiful golden-brown crust, making these halloumi chunks so damn tasty.

To make 1 portion

1 potato, diced

200g frozen spinach

2 tsp curry powder

100g halloumi, diced

Olive oil

Salt and pepper

To cook

Season and pan-fry the diced potato in a splash of olive oil over a medium heat for about 10 minutes until it starts to soften, then add the frozen spinach and a teaspoon of curry powder. As the spinach melts, grab a separate pan and pan-fry the halloumi in a splash of olive oil with a teaspoon of curry powder over a medium heat for about 5 minutes. Once golden brown, mix with the potato and spinach, season to taste and serve.

Make it vegan

To make this dish vegan, substitute the halloumi with a plant-based alternative or firm tofu.

CORONATION CHICKPEAS

The texture of oven-roasted chickpeas makes them so delicious and moreish. One of my favourite ways to roast them is in a splash of olive oil and some curry powder, as I've done here to create this coronation chickpea dish.

To make 1 portion

200g chickpeas (from a 400g tin), drained

1 tsp curry powder for the chickpeas, plus ½ tsp for the sauce

½ mug of basmati rice

1 mug of water

Pinch of ground turmeric

Small handful of chopped coriander

2 tbsp crème fraîche

Small handful of flaked almonds

Olive oil

Salt and pepper

To cook

Preheat your oven to 190°C/gas mark 5.

Put the chickpeas into an ovenproof dish and add a generous glug of olive oil, a teaspoon of curry powder and a pinch of salt and pepper. Mix and then roast in the oven for about 25 minutes until golden brown.

Meanwhile, put the rice, water and a pinch of turmeric into a saucepan and cook over a medium heat with the lid on for about 7 minutes until all the water is absorbed and the rice is cooked.

Then fluff the rice with a fork and mix in the chopped coriander.

To make the sauce, mix the crème fraîche with half a teaspoon of curry powder and a pinch each of salt and pepper.

Serve the rice with a dollop of the sauce, topped with the chickpeas and garnished with flaked almonds.

Make it vegan
To make this dish vegan, swap the crème fraîche for a plant-based crème fraîche or plant-based yogurt.

BLACK BEAN MOUSSAKA

By swapping mince for black beans, you can make a great vegetarian moussaka without compromising on flavour. This has to be in my top ten vegetarian dishes of all time. You don't have to stack it up as I've done here though, just layer it in an ovenproof dish if that's easier for you.

To make 1 portion

½ onion, sliced

Pinch of cumin seeds

200g black beans (from a 400g tin), drained

200g chopped tomatoes (from a 400g tin)

3 slices of aubergine

1 tsp butter

1 tsp plain flour

200ml milk

Small handful of grated Cheddar cheese

1 egg

Olive oil

Salt and pepper

To cook

Preheat your oven to 190°C/gas mark 5.

Pan-fry the onion in a splash of olive oil over a medium heat for a few minutes. Season and add a pinch of cumin seeds, then continue to fry for a few more minutes. Add the black beans and the chopped tomatoes and simmer for about 10 minutes until the sauce has thickened. Season to taste and set to one side.

Meanwhile, in a separate pan, season and fry the aubergine in a splash of olive oil over a medium heat for a few minutes on each side. Set to one side.

In a saucepan, melt the butter over a medium heat, add the flour and cook for a minute, stirring continuously. Slowly add the milk, stirring all the time, and when a lump-free sauce has formed, remove from the heat, stir in the cheese, crack in the egg and mix everything together well.

Assemble the moussaka in an ovenproof dish. Start with an aubergine slice, add a tablespoon of the white sauce, and then a couple of tablespoons of black beans. Repeat the layers. Top with the third slice of aubergine and finish with a final tablespoon of white sauce.

Bake in the oven for about 20 minutes until the cheese sauce is bubbling, then serve.

PULLED BBQ MUSHROOMS

Shredded sticky BBQ mushrooms on a toasted bun with sweet potato fries and slaw . . . This is a hunger-busting plate of pub grub.

To make 1 portion

1 sweet potato, cut into chips

1 portobello mushroom

1 red onion, sliced

Big squeeze of tomato ketchup

1 tsp smoked paprika

1 tsp muscovado sugar

Small wedge of red cabbage, shredded

½ carrot, cut into matchsticks

1 tbsp mayonnaise

Bread roll, sliced and toasted

Olive oil

Salt and pepper

To cook

Preheat your oven to 190°C/gas mark 5.

Place the sweet potato chips on a lined baking tray, drizzle with olive oil and season with salt and pepper, then cook in the oven for about 30 minutes, turning occasionally.

Meanwhile, tear the mushroom into pieces with your hands and pan-fry with half the sliced onion in a splash of olive oil over a medium heat for about 10 minutes until the onions start to caramelise. Add a big squeeze of ketchup, the paprika and the sugar, then simmer for a few minutes until the sauce goes a dark brown colour.

To make the slaw, mix the shredded cabbage with the carrot and the remaining sliced red onion, then add a tablespoon of mayo and a pinch of pepper.

Serve the pulled BBQ mushrooms on a toasted bun with the slaw and sweet potato chips.

Make it vegan

To make this dish vegan, substitute the mayonnaise with vegan mayonnaise, or leave it out altogether.

CABBAGE POTSTICKERS

It's taken me five books to actually write my potsticker recipe. It was too difficult to come up with an easy way to fold them into an elegant shape, so in the end I settled for just folding them in half and scrunching the ends together.

To make 1 portion

A small wedge of Savoy cabbage, finely shredded

1 garlic clove, crushed

Splash of sesame oil

40g plain flour, plus extra for dusting

25g water

Splash of soy sauce, plus extra for dipping

Salt and pepper

To cook

Pan-fry the shredded cabbage and the crushed garlic in a splash of sesame oil over a medium heat for a few minutes. Season with salt and pepper, add a splash of soy sauce and continue to cook for a further couple of minutes until the cabbage is cooked and soft. Transfer the cabbage to a bowl to cool but keep the dirty pan for frying the potstickers later.

In a bowl mix together the flour and water along with a pinch of salt to create a dough. Knead on a floured worktop for a few minutes until smooth, then cut into 6 smaller balls. Dust each ball with flour and roll into a rough circle about 7cm in diameter. Trim to create a neat circle (either using a cookie cutter, knife or scissors) and then leave on the dusted worktop to dry out a little and firm up.

Turn the dough circles over, so the drier side is underneath. Add a teaspoon of cabbage filling to each, fold them in half and scrunch the edges together to create a seal. Then pan-fry in the same pan that you cooked the cabbage with the lid on for a few minutes. Once the bottoms are golden brown and the tops are cooked, remove from the pan and serve with a soy sauce dip.

LENTIL SOUP

This substantial lentil soup – a hearty and warming hug in a bowl – is perfect for a winter's day.

To make I portion

1 onion, diced

1 garlic clove, sliced

200g green lentils (from a 400g tin), plus half the liquid

½ vegetable stock cube

1 tsp Dijon mustard

Splash of single cream

Olive oil

Salt and pepper

To cook

Pan-fry the onion and garlic in a splash of olive oil over a medium heat for a few minutes. Just before the garlic starts to brown, add the lentils, along with their liquid (half the liquid from the tin), crumble in the stock cube and add the mustard. Simmer for about 5 minutes, adding a splash of water to loosen it to soup consistency, then season to taste with salt and pepper.

Blitz half of the soup in a food processor or blender, adding a splash more water if needed, then return it to the pan with the unblended lentils. Serve in a bowl with a splash of cream and a drizzle of olive oil.

Make it vegan

Swap the single cream for vegan cream or leave out the cream.

CARROT & CORIANDER SALAD

The trick to this salad is to use fresh coriander, and marinate everything in lime juice: squeezing fresh lime over the salad and leaving it for 10 minutes means the raw onion 'cooks' lightly in the acidity and softens up to create a nice mellow flavour.

To make 1 portion

Handful of thinly sliced red cabbage

¼ red onion, thinly sliced

Handful of chopped coriander

¼ carrot, cut into thin matchsticks

½ lime

Olive oil

Salt and pepper

To make

Mix the cabbage and onion in a bowl with the coriander and carrot. Squeeze over the lime juice, add a splash of olive oil and a pinch each of salt and pepper, then leave it to rest for at least 10 minutes before serving.

LEEK & BLUE CHEESE TART

Sweet sliced leeks make a great filling for this tart, and create a lovely base for the blue cheese topping. There's no pre-cooking required, so this is extremely simple and delicious 3-ingredient cooking.

To make 1 portion

15 x 15cm square of puff pastry

¼ leek, very thinly sliced

Small handful of blue cheese chunks

Olive oil

Salt and pepper

To cook

Preheat your oven to 190°C/gas mark 5 and line a tray with greaseproof paper.

Lay the pastry on the lined baking tray and score a 1cm border all the way round. Prick the middle of the pastry multiple times with a fork, inside the scored line.

Lightly coat the thinly sliced leeks in a tiny splash of olive oil and season with a pinch each of salt and pepper. Pile the leeks into the middle of the pastry, rub a small amount of olive oil onto the edges of the pastry and bake for 15–20 minutes until the pastry is golden brown. Remove from the oven, top with blue cheese and serve.

CAPONATA

This is a fresh and vibrant Italian dish made with capers and a splash of the caper brine to create a zingy plate of food that packs a punch.

To make 1 portion

¼ aubergine, roughly diced

½ red onion, roughly sliced

1 garlic clove, sliced

Pinch of dried oregano

1 tomato, roughly chopped

Small handful of capers

Big splash of liquid from the caper jar

Handful of spinach

½ mug of couscous

½ mug of boiling water

Olive oil

Salt and pepper

To cook

Start by pan-frying the aubergine in a dry pan over a medium heat for a few minutes until it starts to colour. Then add a splash of olive oil, the onion, garlic and a pinch of oregano. Fry for a few minutes until the garlic starts to colour, then add the tomato. Continue frying for a few more minutes before adding the capers and a big splash of the caper brine. Simmer for a couple of minutes, remove from the heat, then add a handful of spinach, allowing it to wilt in the heat of the pan, and season to taste.

In a bowl, mix together the couscous, a pinch of salt and pepper and the boiling water. Leave to stand for a few minutes then fluff with a fork and serve with the caponata.

CHEESE SOUFFLÉ OMELETTE

This is a breakfast for a special day. It only takes 5 more minutes than a normal omelette but the final result will blow your mind. My top tip is to be brave and try to make yours slightly underdone in the middle. Just give it a try!

To make 1 portion

3 eggs

Handful of finely grated Cheddar cheese (if possible use a Microplane or very fine grater), plus extra for garnishing

Olive oil

Pepper

To cook

Preheat the grill to high.

Separate the eggs and whisk the egg whites in a bowl until they form soft peaks. Then in a separate bowl mix the egg yolks with a pinch of pepper and a handful of very finely grated Cheddar.

Gently fold the egg whites and yolks together, then pour into a small oiled preheated frying pan over a medium heat. Cook for exactly 1 minute then cook the top under the grill for another minute.

Fold the omelette in half, garnish with cheese and serve.

CASHEWS IN BLACK BEAN SAUCE

Tinned black beans are a great addition to any store cupboard. They last for ages, they're ready to use at a moment's notice, and best of all they are already cooked so will save you time in the kitchen.

To make 1 portion

½ onion, roughly diced

½ green pepper, roughly diced

Splash of sesame oil

1 garlic clove, sliced

Squeeze of honey

Pinch of dried chilli flakes

200g black beans (from a 400g tin), plus ½ the liquid from the tin

½ vegetable stock cube

Generous glug of soy sauce

Small handful of cashew nuts

Salt and pepper

To cook

Pan-fry the onion and green pepper in a splash of sesame oil over a medium heat for a couple of minutes. Add the garlic and fry for a few more minutes until the garlic starts to colour. Next add the honey, chilli flakes, black beans, liquid from the black bean tin and the stock cube. Simmer for a few minutes to thicken the sauce, season to taste, then finish with a generous glug of soy sauce, a small handful of cashew nuts and a little more black pepper.

Make it vegan
To make this dish vegan, substitute the honey with agave nectar or maple syrup.

BEETROOT LATKES

These latkes are deliciously crispy and the toasted cumin seeds give them an amazing flavour – perfect for dipping in cool mint yogurt.

To make 1 portion

1 raw beetroot

Pinch of cumin seeds

1 egg

2 tbsp gram flour (chickpea flour)

1 tbsp yogurt

Pinch of dried mint

Olive oil

Salt and pepper

To cook

Grate the beetroot into a bowl and add the cumin seeds, egg and gram flour, season then mix. Heat a pan and dollop in the mixture, then fry over a medium heat in a splash of oil for about 3 minutes on each side.

Mix the yogurt with the dried mint and then serve with the beetroot latkes.

THAI-STYLE RED CURRY NOODLES

Sriracha is a huge shortcut ingredient when you crave spicy food. There's no need for chillies and endless spices: just add a squirt of sriracha and you are minutes away from a simple £1 Thai-inspired curry.

To make 1 portion

½ red onion, sliced

1 garlic clove, sliced

Splash of sesame oil

100ml coconut milk (from a 400ml tin)

100ml water

Big squirt of sriracha

Small handful of udon noodles (pre-cooked, from a pouch)

A few broccoli stalks

Pinch of sesame seeds

Soy sauce

To cook

Pan-fry the onion and garlic in the sesame oil over a medium heat for a few minutes until the garlic starts to brown. Add the coconut milk, water and sriracha. Simmer for a minute, then add the noodles and broccoli. Continue to simmer for about 5 minutes until the broccoli is cooked.

Transfer to a bowl, sprinkle with the sesame seeds and add a splash of soy sauce.

HALLOUMI TIKKA MASALA

Halloumi is the perfect substitute for chicken in this classic takeaway dish. By pan-frying the halloumi with curry powder, you can replicate that delicious charred effect created by the tandoor oven.

To make 1 portion

½ onion, sliced

2 tsp curry powder

200g chopped tomatoes (from a 400g tin)

100g halloumi, cut into cubes

Splash of single cream

Olive oil

Salt and pepper

To cook

Start by pan-frying the onion in a splash of olive oil over a medium heat for about 5 minutes before adding half the curry powder and chopped tomatoes. Season to taste, then simmer for another 5 minutes.

Meanwhile, in a separate pan, fry the halloumi in a splash of oil for a few minutes, turning occasionally. Then add the remaining curry powder and continue to fry for a few more minutes until nicely coloured.

Add the halloumi to the sauce, then finish with a splash of cream before serving.

SPINACH ORECCHIETTE

Frozen spinach is very different from fresh spinach: it gives a dish much greater depth of flavour. I always keep some in the freezer to be used at a moment's notice.

To make 1 portion

Handful of dried orecchiette pasta

3 blocks of frozen spinach (about 50g)

2 garlic cloves, sliced

Big glug of single cream

Small handful of grated Parmesan cheese

Olive oil

Salt and pepper

To cook

Bring a saucepan of salted water to the boil, add the pasta and cook until al dente.

Meanwhile, defrost the spinach in a dry frying pan over a medium heat, and when it is almost fully defrosted, add a glug of olive oil and the garlic. Fry for a few minutes until the garlic starts to colour, then add the cream, season with salt and pepper and simmer for a minute.

Drain the pasta (retaining a little of the cooking water). Add the pasta and a splash of the cooking water to the pan of spinach and stir to combine. Serve drizzled with olive oil and scattered with the grated Parmesan.

PEPERONATA SWEET POTATOES

This is a mega-speedy jacket potato filling for you to try out at home. Grab a jar of roasted peppers and follow these steps to create an unusual but delicious dish.

To make 1 portion

1 sweet potato

A few roasted peppers from a jar, plus a splash of the oil

Squirt of sriracha

Small handful of chopped coriander

1 tbsp crème fraîche

Salt and pepper

To cook

Preheat the oven to 200°C/gas mark 6.

Cook the sweet potato by piercing it a few times with a fork and baking in the oven for about 40 minutes. You could also microwave it for about 10 minutes.

While the potato is cooking, make the filling. Slice the peppers and mix them with a splash of oil from the jar, a squirt of sriracha, the chopped coriander and a pinch each of salt and pepper.

When the sweet potato is cooked, slice it open, fluff the middle with a fork, season with salt and pepper, then add a dollop of crème fraîche and the pepper filling.

Make it vegan

To make this dish vegan, substitute the crème fraîche with vegan crème fraîche or vegan yogurt.

MUSHROOM STROGANOFF

Here's a super-speedy vegan mushroom stroganoff for you to try. All the classic flavours are there, such as garlic and paprika, but in this dish the creaminess comes from a combination of oat milk and flour.

To make 1 portion

½ mug of brown rice

1 mug of water

1 portobello mushroom, cut into 1cm-thick slices

1 garlic clove, sliced

½ tsp paprika

1 tsp plain flour

150ml oat milk (or any milk substitute)

Small handful of spinach

Olive oil

Salt and pepper

To cook

Put the rice and water in a saucepan and cook over a medium heat with the lid on for about 15 minutes, until all the water has been absorbed and the rice is cooked.

Meanwhile, pan-fry the sliced mushroom in a splash of olive oil over a medium heat for a few minutes. When the mushroom is almost cooked, season with salt and pepper and add the garlic, along with a splash more olive oil and continue to fry until the garlic starts to brown. Add the paprika and flour to the pan and stir for another minute, then gradually pour in the milk, stirring constantly. Simmer for a few minutes until the sauce thickens. Add the spinach and allow it to wilt, then remove from the heat. Season to taste and serve with the rice.

LEEK & MUSHROOM POT PIE

A creamy leek sauce with mushrooms and a crispy pastry lid . . . this is food that gives you a nice warm hug on a cold day.

To make 1 portion

1 leek, sliced

A few mushrooms, sliced

1 tsp plain flour

1 tsp Dijon mustard

200ml milk

10cm diameter circle of puff pastry

1 egg, beaten

Olive oil

Salt and pepper

To cook

Preheat your oven to 190°C/gas mark 5.

Season and pan-fry the leeks and mushrooms in a splash of olive oil over a medium heat for about 10 minutes until cooked. Then add the flour and mustard and continue cooking for a minute, stirring constantly, before slowly adding the milk, stirring all the time, to create a sauce. Simmer for a few more minutes to thicken a little, then transfer to a round ovenproof dish about 10cm in diameter.

Place the pastry lid on top of the filling, brush with the beaten egg and cook in the oven for about 30 minutes until golden brown.

Make it vegan
Use plant-based milk, vegan pastry and don't brush with egg.

AUBERGINE THERMIDOR

One of the most expensive dishes you'll ever see on a menu is lobster thermidor, so I took this as a challenge to create my very own £1 version. For me, the coolest part of lobster thermidor is that you put it all back into the shell, so aubergine is the perfect vegetable for this meat-free version.

To make 1 portion

½ aubergine

½ onion, diced

1 garlic clove, sliced

1 tsp plain flour

100ml milk

Pinch of smoked paprika

1 tsp English mustard

Small handful of grated mature Cheddar cheese

Small handful of breadcrumbs (grated stale bread)

Pinch of dried parsley

Olive oil

Salt and pepper

To cook

Preheat your oven to 190°C/gas mark 5.

Cut the flesh of the aubergine in a criss-cross pattern, being careful not to cut through the skin. Scoop out the chunks of aubergine using a spoon, then season and fry in a splash of olive oil along with the onion and garlic over a medium heat. After a few minutes, just as the garlic is starting to colour, add the teaspoon of flour and continue to fry for a further minute, stirring continuously, before adding the milk, little by little, stirring all the time.

Once all the milk is added and a lump-free sauce has been created, remove from the heat and add a pinch of paprika, the mustard and the grated Cheddar. Stir until the cheese has melted into the sauce, then pour the sauce into the hollowed-out aubergine skin.

Mix the breadcrumbs with a splash of olive oil, a pinch of dried parsley, and a pinch each of salt and pepper, then sprinkle on top of the filled aubergine. Place the aubergine on a baking tray and cook in the oven for about 20 minutes until the sauce is bubbling and the breadcrumbs are golden brown.

Make it vegan
To make this dish vegan, substitute the milk and cheese with plant-based alternatives.

BLINIS

Homemade blinis taste so much better than shop-bought, and they can be topped with anything. I like the peppery combination of horseradish and radish, with a bit of rocket and crème fraîche, but this could be a great opportunity to use up any leftovers in the fridge.

To make 1 portion (5 blinis)

100g cold mashed potato

1 medium egg

50ml milk

50g self-raising flour

A couple of radishes, sliced

1 tsp creamed horseradish

2 tbsp crème fraîche

A few rocket leaves

Olive oil

Salt and pepper

To cook

Mix the mashed potato, egg, milk and self-raising flour in a bowl until it forms a thick batter, then season with a pinch each of salt and pepper.

Heat a glug of olive oil in a frying pan over a medium heat, then add dollops of the batter (the mixture should make about 5 blinis). Fry for a few minutes on each side until golden brown.

Next make the topping. Mix the sliced radishes with the horseradish and crème fraîche, and season with salt and pepper. Scatter a few rocket leaves onto the blinis and spoon over the topping.

CHARRED PEPPERS & BREADCRUMBS

I love to cook with breadcrumbs: they are cheap and versatile, and they elevate a dish by adding texture. Whenever I have leftover bread, I just let it go dry, stick it in the blender to make breadcrumbs (you could also grate it), then store the crumbs in jars.

To make 1 portion

1½ peppers, in contrasting colours, cut into quarters

½ red onion, finely diced

1 garlic clove, sliced

Handful of breadcrumbs

Small handful of parsley, chopped

Olive oil

Salt and pepper

To cook

Preheat your grill to high.

Cook the peppers under the grill skin-side up until soft and slightly charred.

Meanwhile, pan-fry the onion in a splash of olive oil over a medium heat for a few minutes, then add the garlic and fry for a few more minutes until the garlic starts to brown. Add the breadcrumbs and a splash more olive oil, and season with salt and pepper. Fry for a couple of minutes, until the breadcrumbs are golden brown, then add the chopped parsley and remove from the heat.

Serve the peppers topped with the fried breadcrumbs.

WELSH RAREBIT & TOMATO PIE

This takes all the ingredients of a Welsh rarebit, including its creamy, cheesy topping – even the toast – and turns them into a delicious pie.

To make 1 portion

75ml single cream

75g grated Cheddar cheese

1 spring onion, sliced

Squeeze of English mustard

Splash of vegan Worcestershire sauce

Pinch of dried oregano

A few slices of stale bread

A few slices of tomato

Salt and pepper

To cook

Preheat your oven to 190°C/gas mark 5.

Grab a bowl and make the sauce by combining the cream, Cheddar cheese, spring onion, mustard, Worcestershire sauce, oregano and a pinch each of salt and pepper.

Layer half the bread, tomato slices and sauce in a round ovenproof dish about 15cm in diameter and repeat with the rest of the bread, tomato and sauce to make two rough layers. Bake in the oven for about 30 minutes, until the cheese is bubbling.

CHANA MASALA

For the ultimate £1 chana masala, make it as hot as you dare and then add the cooling yogurt, mint and pea sauce.

To make 1 portion

½ red onion, sliced

1 garlic clove, sliced

1 tsp curry powder

Pinch of dried chilli flakes

200g chickpeas (from a 400g tin), drained

200g chopped tomatoes (from a 400g tin)

Small handful of frozen peas

1 tbsp yogurt

Pinch of dried mint

Olive oil

Salt and pepper

To cook

Season and pan-fry the onion in a splash of olive oil over a medium heat for a few minutes. Then add the garlic and continue to fry for a few minutes until the garlic starts to colour. At this point add the curry powder, chilli flakes and the chickpeas, and fry for a couple of minutes. Add the chopped tomatoes then simmer for about 10 minutes. Season to taste.

While the chana masala is simmering, defrost the peas under a hot tap, then mix with the yogurt and dried mint.

Serve the chana masala with a dollop of the cooling yogurt, mint and pea sauce.

Make it vegan
To make this dish vegan, substitute the yogurt with vegan yogurt.

PINEAPPLE FRIED RICE

My favourite part of this dish is the caramelisation of the natural sugars contained in the pineapple. The added bonus is that the pineapple skin is used as a bowl, which not only looks spectacular but also saves on the washing-up.

To make 1 portion

½ mug of brown rice

1 mug of water

½ pineapple

Sesame oil

1 spring onion, chopped

½ carrot, diced

1 egg

Splash of soy sauce

Salt and pepper

To cook

Start by putting the brown rice and water into a saucepan and simmering over a medium heat for about 10 minutes until all the water has been absorbed and the rice is cooked. Then set to one side to cool.

Meanwhile, cut the flesh of the pineapple in a criss-cross pattern then scoop it out with a spoon. Discard the core of the pineapple, chop the rest into chunks and pan-fry in a splash of sesame oil over a medium heat for a few minutes until slightly caramelised. Remove from the pan and set to one side for later.

Next pan-fry the spring onion and carrot in a splash of sesame oil over a medium heat for a few minutes until softened. Add the rice and continue to fry for a few minutes before pushing to one side of the pan and cracking an egg into the empty side. When the egg is about 80 per cent cooked, scramble and mix with the rice. Add the caramelised pineapple chunks, a splash of sesame oil and a splash of soy sauce. Season to taste and serve in the hollowed-out pineapple skin.

CHICKPEA & SAAG MASH

Mashed potato works great as a blank canvas for creating interesting dishes. Here, I've taken the famous saag aloo potato and spinach dish and turned it into a luxurious curried creamy mash topped with crunchy roasted chickpeas.

To make 1 portion

200g chickpeas (from a 400g tin), drained

1 tsp curry powder for the chickpeas, 1 tsp curry powder for the mash

1 large potato, peeled and roughly diced

200g frozen spinach, defrosted

Olive oil

Salt and pepper

To cook

Preheat your oven to 190°C/ gas mark 5.

Put the chickpeas into an ovenproof dish and add a generous glug of olive oil, a teaspoon of curry powder and a pinch each of salt and pepper. Mix and then roast in the oven for about 25 minutes until golden brown.

Meanwhile, cook the diced potato in a pan of salted boiling water for about 10 minutes until soft, then drain and mash. Stir in the spinach, a glug of olive oil, a teaspoon of curry powder, and then season with salt and pepper.

Serve the mash topped with the chickpeas and a drizzle of olive oil.

APPLE & STILTON SLAW

Crispy Stilton croutons piled with a tasty creamy slaw, then topped with slices of apple . . . It's not really a salad but it's definitely more than just a coleslaw.

To make 1 portion

Small handful of crumbled Stilton

A couple of slices of baguette

½ red onion, sliced

Wedge of red cabbage, sliced

½ carrot, cut into matchsticks

1 tbsp crème fraîche

1 tsp Dijon mustard

A few slices of apple

Salt and pepper

To cook

Preheat your oven to 190°C/gas mark 5.

Pile the crumbled Stilton onto the baguette slices and cook on a baking tray for about 10 minutes until the bread is crispy and the cheese has melted.

Meanwhile, to make the slaw, grab a bowl and mix together the onion, cabbage, carrot, crème fraîche and Dijon mustard, then season to taste. Serve with the Stilton croutons and top with a few slices of apple.

PORTOBELLO KIEV

It's difficult to stuff a mushroom with garlic butter – trust me, I've tried. Then I came up with this: my mushroom Kiev. The breadcrumb coating gets nice and crispy, then you add the garlic butter as a sauce at the end. Genius!

To make 1 portion

1 portobello mushroom

Small handful of breadcrumbs (grated stale bread)

Small handful of chopped parsley, plus a pinch for the topping

1 large potato, peeled

3 garlic cloves

3 tbsp butter

Olive oil

Salt and pepper

To cook

Preheat your oven to 190°C/gas mark 5.

Rub the mushroom with olive oil. Mix the breadcrumbs in a bowl with a splash of olive oil, the pinch of chopped parsley, and some salt and pepper. Put the mushroom on a baking tray, top the mushroom with the breadcrumb and parsley mixture and cook in the oven for about 15 minutes, until the breadcrumbs are golden brown.

Meanwhile, cut the potato into rough chunks, add to a saucepan of salted boiling water and cook for about 15 minutes until tender, then drain, return to the pan, mash with a glug of olive oil and season with a pinch each of salt and pepper.

To make the sauce, pan-fry the garlic in a splash of olive oil over a medium heat for a few minutes until sizzling (but not browned), add the butter and fry for a few more minutes, adding the parsley just before the garlic starts to brown. Serve the sauce drizzled over the baked mushroom and mashed potato.

Make it vegan
Use olive oil instead of butter.

HARISSA-BAKED AUBERGINE

Criss-cross your aubergine to get maximum flavour inside, then just relax and let the oven do the rest of the work. When it's ready, add creamy yogurt and sweet honey to contrast with the harissa spices.

To make 1 portion

½ aubergine

2 tsp harissa spices

200g chopped tomatoes (from a 400g tin)

1 tbsp yogurt

1 tbsp honey

Small handful of flaked almonds

Olive oil

Salt and pepper

To cook

Preheat your oven to 190°C/gas mark 5.

Cut the flesh of the aubergine in a criss-cross pattern, being careful not to cut through the skin. Rub 1 teaspoon of harissa spices into the aubergine, along with a pinch each of salt and pepper.

Pour the chopped tomatoes into an ovenproof dish, add a splash of water and the remaining teaspoon of harissa spices, along with a pinch each of salt and pepper. Place the aubergine in the dish and drizzle with olive oil. Bake for about 45 minutes until the chopped tomatoes have reduced and the aubergine is soft and cooked. Remove from the oven, add a tablespoon each of yogurt and honey, then garnish with flaked almonds.

Make it vegan

To make this dish vegan, substitute the honey with agave nectar or maple syrup, and the yogurt with plant-based yogurt.

HOT TABBOULEH

Bulgur wheat is economical and delicious but in the UK it is really underused, so I've created a simple dish that you can make easily and which will hopefully give you the inspiration and confidence to use it more. Even better, you'll fall in love with this amazing ingredient.

To make 1 portion

Handful of bulgur wheat

2 spring onions, roughly chopped

½ red pepper, diced

Olive oil

Salt and pepper

To cook

Start by cooking the bulgur wheat in salted boiling water for about 12 minutes until soft, then drain.

Meanwhile, pan-fry the spring onions and pepper in a generous glug of olive oil and a pinch each of salt and pepper for about 5 minutes. Then add the bulgur wheat and mix everything together. Season to taste, then serve.

ULTIMATE £1 CORN ON THE COB

Don't be scared of cooking corn on the cob, it's really easy and you don't even need to boil it – just chuck it into a dry frying pan. I'm not sure why people make it so difficult.

To make 1 portion

1 corn on the cob

1 tomato, roughly diced

Squirt of sriracha

Small handful of chopped coriander

1 tbsp crème fraîche

Olive oil

Salt and pepper

To cook

Rub the corn with a tiny amount of olive oil and then toast in a dry frying pan over a medium heat, turning every few minutes until slightly charred all the way round.

To make the salsa, mix the roughly diced tomato with a squirt of sriracha, the chopped coriander, a splash of olive oil and a pinch each of salt and pepper.

Once the corn is cooked, serve with a big dollop of crème fraîche and then spoon over the salsa.

Make it vegan

To make this dish vegan, substitute the crème fraîche with a plant-based crème fraîche or yogurt.

BUTTERNUT SQUASH POLENTA

This warming and filling dish proves you can have a tasty, hearty meal on a budget. I like to scatter over a few roasted butternut squash seeds for extra texture, then drizzle the polenta with the oil from the roasting tray.

To make 1 portion

Handful of cubed butternut squash, plus some squash seeds

1 tsp smoked paprika

¼ mug of polenta

1¼ mugs of milk

Olive oil

Salt and pepper

To cook

Preheat your oven to 190°C/gas mark 5.

Throw the cubed butternut squash into a roasting tray, add the paprika and toss with a generous glug of olive oil and a pinch each of salt and pepper. Roast in the oven for about 30 minutes, throwing in a few butternut squash seeds halfway through, until the butternut squash is cooked and slightly charred. Remove from the oven and set to one side while you make the polenta.

Put the polenta and milk in a saucepan and bring to the boil while continuously stirring. Simmer gently for about 7 minutes, stirring all the time, until thick, then remove from the heat. Season with salt and pepper and pour into a bowl.

Top the polenta with the roasted butternut squash and the seeds, then drizzle over the paprika-infused oil from the roasting tray.

Make it vegan
To make this dish vegan, use plant-based milk.

CARAMELISED ONION QUICHE

Onions bring so much depth of flavour to a dish like this. They are my number-one ingredient for adding oomph when cooking on a budget. Just fry them slowly and the natural sugars start to caramelise, creating a tasty filling for your quiche.

To make 1 portion

1 red onion, sliced

20 x 20cm square of shop-bought shortcrust pastry

3 eggs

Splash of milk

Small handful of grated Cheddar cheese

Olive oil

Salt and pepper

To cook

Preheat your oven to 190°C/gas mark 5.

Season and pan-fry the onion gently in a splash of olive oil over a low-medium heat for about 10 to 15 minutes, until it starts to caramelise.

Remove the pan from the heat and allow the onion to cool while you line a round ovenproof dish about 15cm in diameter with the shortcrust pastry. Trim the edges to make a neat pastry case, then prepare your filling.

Crack the eggs into a bowl, add the milk, caramelised onion, grated cheese and a pinch each of salt and pepper. Pour the filling mixture into the pastry-lined dish and bake in the oven for about 20 minutes until the filling is set and golden brown on top.

AUBERGINE PARMIGIANA

Griddling the aubergine first gives this dish a slightly smoky flavour. And here's a trick for you: line your dish with tin foil so you can lift the parmigiana out in one piece and see the layers.

To make 1 portion

1 red onion, very thinly sliced

1 garlic clove, thinly sliced

200g chopped tomatoes (from a 400g tin)

A few pinches of dried oregano

½ aubergine, cut into slices

Handful of breadcrumbs

Handful of grated Parmesan cheese

Olive oil

Salt and pepper

To cook

Preheat your oven to 190°C/gas mark 5.

Pan-fry the onion in a splash of olive oil over a medium heat for about 5 minutes until soft, then add the garlic and continue to fry for a few minutes until it starts to colour. At this point add the chopped tomatoes, a pinch of dried oregano, a splash of water, and a pinch each of salt and pepper, then simmer for about 10 minutes.

Meanwhile, brush the aubergine slices with a bit of olive oil and sprinkle with salt and pepper before griddling (or pan-frying) over a medium heat for about 5 minutes on each side until nicely coloured.

Next, mix the breadcrumbs with a pinch of oregano, most of the Parmesan (keeping a little bit to add at the end), a splash of olive oil and a pinch each of salt and pepper.

Grab an ovenproof dish about 15 x 10cm and line it with foil. Start with a layer of aubergine (you might have to cut them to size), then a layer of tomato sauce, then a layer of breadcrumbs, and repeat, finishing with a layer of breadcrumbs.

Bake in the oven for about 30 minutes then serve with a sprinkle of grated Parmesan.

Make it vegan

To make this dish vegan, substitute the Parmesan with a vegan alternative.

COCONUT DAAL

By using coconut milk, you can create a luxurious and creamy daal that is totally vegan. This is a lovely, comforting dish of food.

To make 1 portion

½ onion, sliced

1 garlic clove, sliced

Handful of red lentils

1 tsp curry powder

200g coconut milk (from 400g tin)

1 mug of water

200g chickpeas (from 400g tin), drained

Small handful of spinach

Olive oil

Salt and pepper

To cook

Grab a saucepan and fry the onion and garlic in a splash of olive oil over a medium heat for about 5 minutes until soft and cooked. Add the lentils and curry powder and stir, coating the lentils in the oil. Next add the coconut milk and the water and simmer for about 15 minutes until the lentils are cooked (adding more water if needed). About 5 minutes before the end of the cooking time, add the chickpeas and season to taste. Just before serving add the spinach, stirring it through so it wilts.

PUTTANESCA BAKE

This recipe takes puttanesca pasta in a whole new direction. The flavours intensify under the grill and when the stringy mozzarella mixes with the sauce it creates a luxurious version of the original dish.

To make 1 portion

Handful of rigatoni pasta

½ red onion, finely sliced

1 garlic clove, sliced

200g chopped tomatoes (from a 400g tin)

A few black olives

Pinch of chilli flakes

Pinch of dried oregano

Slice of a mozzarella ball

Olive oil

Salt and pepper

To cook

Cook the pasta in a pan of salted boiling water as per the instructions on the packet, then drain.

Pan-fry the onion in a splash of olive oil over a medium heat for a few minutes. Add the garlic and continue to fry for a few more minutes until the garlic starts to colour. Add the chopped tomatoes, olives, chilli flakes, oregano, and a pinch each of salt and pepper, then simmer for about 10 minutes.

Preheat the grill to high. Add the cooked pasta to the sauce, transfer everything to an ovenproof dish if your frying pan is not oven proof, then top with the mozzarella slice and cook for a few minutes under the grill until the cheese is bubbling and starting to colour.

Make it vegan

To make this dish vegan, substitute the mozzarella with a vegan alternative.

VEGETABLE TERRINE

The outside of this veggie terrine looks delicate and intricate, but really it's just some thin, slightly overlapping slices of courgette. To get your courgettes extra thin, just use a vegetable peeler – people will think you've got amazing knife skills.

To make 1 portion

A few mini potatoes

A few asparagus spears

1 spring onion, sliced

½ courgette

3 tbsp cream cheese

A few pieces of roasted red pepper from a jar

A few pieces of roasted yellow pepper from a jar

A few slices of bread

Olive oil

Salt and pepper

To cook

Cook the potatoes in a saucepan of salted boiling water until tender.

While the potatoes are cooking, add the asparagus to the potato pan and let them simmer with the potatoes for a few minutes until cooked, then remove with tongs and set to one side.

Drain the potatoes, tip them back into the pan, season with salt and pepper and roughly mash with a fork, then stir in the spring onion and a splash of olive oil, and allow to cool.

Grab a small rectangular dish about 10 x 5cm and line it with cling film.

Slice the courgette lengthways really thinly with a vegetable peeler then lay the slices inside the dish, overlapping them slightly to create a striped effect. Lay a slice sideways at each end, too, so the dish is fully lined.

Spread 2 tablespoons of the cream cheese into the terrine to create the first layer, smoothing it down with the back of a spoon, then lay the asparagus on the cream cheese, pushing the spears into the cream cheese slightly. Cover with another thin layer of the remaining tablespoon of cream cheese. Next, add a layer of red pepper, then the mashed potato, and finish with a layer of yellow pepper. Fold the ends of the courgette strips and the edges of the cling film over the top and chill for at least one hour, then unwrap and turn out the terrine and serve with bread.

Make it vegan

Swap the cream cheese for vegan cream cheese.

PIZZA FRITTATA

I love pizza. All the flavours go together perfectly, so I thought I'd try them in a frittata – and it works! For an extra punch, I've used sun-dried tomatoes here instead of fresh ones, and fried the frittata in a splash of the oil that comes with them.

To make 1 portion

3 eggs

A few sun-dried tomatoes, plus a splash of the oil

A few chunks of torn mozzarella

Pinch of dried oregano

Salt and pepper

To cook

Crack the eggs into a bowl and beat together. Season with salt and pepper, then fry in a pan in a splash of the sun-dried tomato oil over a medium heat for a few minutes until the bottom is cooked.

Preheat the grill to high. Place the sun-dried tomatoes and mozzarella chunks on top of the eggs. Sprinkle over the oregano, then cook under the grill for a few minutes until the eggs are done and the mozzarella has melted.

AUBERGINE PHO

The sweet and spicy aubergine in this pho soup adds flavour intensity and creates a delicious broth to slurp up those noodles with.

To make 1 portion

200ml water

1 vegetable stock cube

¼ aubergine, diced

¼ red onion, diced

Sesame oil

1 garlic clove, thinly sliced

Pinch of dried chilli flakes

Honey

Soy sauce

¼ pak choi

1 sheet of rice noodles

To cook

Bring the water to the boil in a saucepan and crumble in the stock cube.

Pan-fry the aubergine and red onion in a splash of sesame oil over a medium heat for about 10 minutes until the onion starts to caramelise. Add the garlic and chilli flakes and continue to fry until the garlic starts to brown. At this point, add a big squeeze of honey, a big glug of soy sauce and another splash of sesame oil. Simmer for a few minutes until it thickens and becomes sticky.

Meanwhile, add the pak choi and noodles to the stock and cook according to the time stated on the noodle packet instructions. Transfer the noodles and pak choi to a bowl, pour over enough stock to cover, then add the sticky aubergine and onion.

Make it vegan
Substitute the honey for golden syrup or maple syrup.

SPICY CHILLI BEAN SPROUTS

This is quick and simple cooking at its best, maybe 5 minutes from start to finish. But the biggest revelation is the toasted sesame seeds. You don't have to toast them but I promise you it's worth it.

To make 1 portion

Small handful of sesame seeds

Splash of sesame oil

1 tbsp tomato purée

Pinch of chilli flakes

1 garlic clove, crushed

1 tsp demerara sugar

Squirt of sriracha

Handful of bean sprouts

Handful of spinach

To cook

Start by toasting the sesame seeds in a dry pan over a medium heat for a few minutes until golden brown. Remove from the pan and set to one side then add a splash of sesame oil, the tomato purée, chilli flakes and crushed garlic. Fry for a few minutes, then add the demerara sugar and sriracha. Once the sugar has dissolved, add the bean sprouts and stir-fry for another few minutes before removing from the heat and mixing in the spinach. Allow the spinach to wilt in the heat of the pan, season to taste, then serve with a drizzle of sesame oil and a garnish of toasted sesame seeds.

FILO BIANCO

This thin and crispy tart is packed with flavour. And the oozy filling works so well with the brittle edges of the filo pastry, creating a lovely contrast in texture. But my favourite thing about this dish is the tiny splashes of Worcestershire sauce that cut through the richness of the cheese and cream.

To make 1 portion

3 sheets of filo pastry

Handful of grated Cheddar cheese

Splash of single cream

A few Tenderstem broccoli florets

Splash of vegan Worcestershire sauce

Olive oil

Pinch of black pepper

To cook

Preheat your oven to 190°C/gas mark 5.

Grab a 12cm heatproof dish or a small frying pan with an ovenproof handle and lay the sheets of filo in the dish or pan so that they overlap in the middle and overhang around the sides of the dish. Scrunch the edges up to create a circular pie case that will contain a filling, and brush lightly with olive oil.

Mix the cheese and single cream in a bowl with the pepper to create a paste, then spoon into the filo pastry case. Top with the broccoli florets, add a few splashes of Worcestershire sauce and bake in the oven for about 20 minutes until the pastry is golden brown.

ROTOLO

Real Italian rotolo is complicated to make – it even has a crazy step where you have to wrap the pasta in a cloth and boil it. I wanted to eat it, but I didn't want to make it, so I had to come up with my own One Pound Meals formula. Here it is.

To make 1 portion

3 tbsp ricotta

2 small handfuls of grated Parmesan

Small handful of spinach

1 fresh lasagne sheet

Big glug of single cream

Small handful of frozen peas

Olive oil

Salt and pepper

To cook

Preheat your oven to 190°C/gas mark 5.

Mix the ricotta with half the grated Parmesan, the spinach (you don't need to wilt the spinach, it will soften as you mix it) and a pinch of salt and pepper. Spread the mixture evenly over the sheet of fresh pasta, then roll the pasta into a sausage shape.

Cut the rolled-up pasta sheet into 2.5cm-thick circles and place in an ovenproof dish cut side up. Add the cream, peas and remaining handful of Parmesan to the dish along with a splash of water, drizzle with olive oil and season with salt and pepper. Bake in the oven for about 15 minutes, then serve.

FRIED TOMATOES & COURGETTES

I love pan-fried tomatoes, simply cooked with olive oil, salt and pepper. But when you add this tangy sauce, it transforms the dish into something special.

To make 1 portion

Small handful of chopped parsley

1 garlic clove

A few slices of red onion

Splash of red wine vinegar

1 tbsp plain flour

Small handful of breadcrumbs (grated stale bread)

A few slices of courgette

1 egg, beaten

1 big tomato, sliced

Olive oil

Salt and pepper

To cook

To make the sauce, put some parsley, a garlic clove and a few slices of red onion into a blender. Next add a splash of red wine vinegar and some olive oil in roughly a 1:4 ratio and blend. If the sauce is too thick, add some more red wine vinegar and olive oil.

Next, season both the flour and the breadcrumbs with salt and pepper. Dust the courgette slices in the seasoned flour, then dip them in the beaten egg, and finally roll in the seasoned breadcrumbs. Pan-fry them in a splash of olive oil over a medium heat for about 3 minutes on each side, or until golden brown.

Once the courgettes are cooked, remove from the pan. Add a splash more olive oil to the pan, if needed, season the tomato slices generously and then pan-fry them for a couple of minutes on each side.

Transfer the pan-fried tomato and courgette slices to a plate, drizzle with the sauce and serve.

Make it vegan
To make this dish vegan, substitute the egg by brushing the vegetables with a little oil before dipping in the bread-crumbs (no need to dust with flour).

POLENTA-CRUSTED AUBERGINE

This is a dish I once had in Spain. It took me a while to figure out how it was actually done because I kept overcomplicating it. Turns out, you just dip the slices of aubergine in the polenta, and the moisture in the aubergine helps it stick. Then all you need to do is pan-fry them.

To make 1 portion

Small handful of polenta

½ aubergine, cut lengthways into 4 slices

Small handful of crumbled goat's cheese

2 tbsp honey

Small handful of pine nuts

Olive oil

Salt and pepper

To cook

Season the polenta and scatter onto a plate, then dip the aubergine slices in the seasoned polenta. Pan-fry the aubergine in a splash of olive oil over a medium heat for a few minutes on each side until golden brown.

Serve with some crumbled goat's cheese, a drizzle of honey and a scattering of pine nuts.

CRISPY POTATO CAESAR SALAD

Crisp up those potatoes to get them extra crunchy and add this quick homemade Caesar dressing to create my tasty £1 version of a Caesar salad that doesn't compromise on flavour.

To make 1 portion

A few small potatoes, skin on

1 tbsp red wine vinegar

1 tbsp mayonnaise

Pinch of dried oregano

A few lettuce leaves

Olive oil

Salt and pepper

To cook

Preheat your oven to 190°C/gas mark 5.

Cook the potatoes in a pan of salted boiling water for about 15 minutes until soft and cooked. Drain and let them steam for a bit to dry out.

Transfer the potatoes to an ovenproof dish and squash each one slightly with the back of a fork to break the skins and expose the fluffy middle. Pour over a generous glug of olive oil, add a pinch of salt and roast for about 40 minutes until crispy.

Meanwhile, to make the dressing, mix together 5 tablespoons of olive oil with the red wine vinegar, mayo, oregano, and a pinch each of salt and pepper. Stir with a fork to combine the ingredients into a creamy sauce, then serve with the lettuce and potatoes.

Make it vegan

To make this dish vegan, substitute the mayo with vegan mayo.

HALLOUMI BAKE

Halloumi is more versatile than you think. Here, I've used it to top this simple, Greek-inspired oven bake. To give it an authentic Mediterranean flavour, try to find Kalamata olives – they have a unique, slightly vinegary taste that transforms this dish by cutting through the sweetness of the tomato.

To make 1 portion

½ red onion, thinly sliced

Small handful of pitted Kalamata olives

200g chopped tomatoes (from a 400g tin)

Pinch of dried oregano

A few slices of halloumi

Olive oil

Salt and pepper

To cook

Preheat your oven to 190°C/gas mark 5.

Pan-fry the onion in a splash of olive oil over a medium heat for a few minutes until soft, then add the olives and chopped tomatoes, along with a pinch each of salt and pepper, and the oregano. Simmer for a couple of minutes, then transfer to an ovenproof dish, top with the halloumi and bake in the oven for 15–20 minutes, until the sauce has thickened and the halloumi starts to turn brown on top. Remove from the oven and serve.

MILK RISOTTO

A while ago, I was curious to find out if you could make risotto with milk. It turns out that it tastes amazing, and adding a pinch of tarragon takes it to a whole new level of deliciousness. But the biggest revelation about my experiment was discovering that plant-based milk makes a super-creamy vegan risotto.

To make 1 portion

½ onion, diced

Handful of arborio rice

300ml milk

Pinch of dried tarragon

A few asparagus spears, cut into thin strips with a potato peeler

Olive oil

Salt and pepper

To cook

Gently pan-fry the onion in a splash of olive oil over a low-medium heat for about 5 minutes, until softened but not coloured. Season with salt and pepper then turn up the heat to medium and add the rice. Stir to coat the rice in the oil, then start adding the milk little by little, about 50ml at a time, while stirring continuously. After 10–15 minutes, once all the milk is added and the rice is cooked, remove the pan from the heat, stir in the tarragon, season to taste and top with the asparagus and a splash of olive oil.

Make it vegan

To make this dish vegan, use a plant-based milk.

AUBERGINE PANGRATTATO

Using stale bread to add extra texture and flavour to a dish is a great money-saving trick from Italy. The breadcrumbs in this dish soak up the lovely garlic oil and create the perfect topping for a simple plate of pasta.

To make 1 portion

Handful of dried linguine

¼ aubergine, diced

1 garlic clove, sliced

Small handful of pine nuts

Small handful of breadcrumbs (grated stale bread)

Small handful of spinach, sliced

Olive oil

Salt and pepper

To cook

Cook the pasta in a pan of salted boiling water as per the instructions on the packet, then drain.

Pan-fry the aubergine in a dry pan over a medium heat for a few minutes until softened and slightly coloured. Then add the garlic and pine nuts, along with a splash of olive oil, and continue frying for a few minutes until the garlic starts to colour. At this point add the breadcrumbs and fry for a few minutes until golden brown, then mix in the sliced spinach. Season to taste and after a minute or so remove from the heat.

Serve the pasta dressed in a splash of olive oil and topped with the aubergine mixture.

CHUNKY BALTI VEG PIE

Just half a teaspoon of turmeric will give your mash a lovely yellow hue and a delicious earthy flavour that will get your mouth watering. Cut your veg extra chunky and this hearty dish will have a bit more bite.

To make 1 portion

1 large potato, cut into large chunks

½ tsp turmeric

½ red onion, cut into large chunks

½ carrot, cut into large chunks

½ courgette, cut into large chunks

1 tsp curry powder

200g chopped tomatoes (from a 400g tin)

Olive oil

Salt and pepper

To cook

Preheat your oven to 190°C/gas mark 5.

Cook the potato chunks in a pan of salted boiling water for about 10 minutes until soft. Then drain and mash with a glug of olive oil, the turmeric and a pinch each of salt and pepper.

Pan-fry the onion, carrot and courgette in a splash of olive oil over a medium heat for about 5 minutes until the onions have softened a bit. Add the curry powder, season and continue to fry for a further minute before adding the chopped tomatoes. Simmer for about 5 minutes. Season to taste, then transfer to a round ovenproof dish and top with the mash. Bake for about 25 minutes until the mash starts to colour, then serve.

AUBERGINE RAGU & POLENTA

There is something so satisfying about a ragu bubbling away on the hob. As the flavours intensify, you know it is going to be well worth the wait. Here, a rich aubergine ragu is served with a creamy polenta to create a nice rustic Italian-style dish.

To make 1 portion

¼ aubergine, diced

½ red onion, diced

1 garlic clove, sliced

200g chopped tomatoes (from a 400g tin)

Pinch of dried oregano

½ mug of polenta

2½ mugs of milk

Olive oil

Salt and pepper

To cook

Pan-fry the aubergine in a splash of olive oil over a medium heat for a few minutes, season with salt and pepper, then add the onion and garlic. Fry for a few more minutes until the garlic starts to brown, then add the chopped tomatoes and oregano and simmer for 10–15 minutes.

Meanwhile, put the polenta and milk in a saucepan and bring to the boil while stirring constantly. Simmer for about 5 minutes until thick, and season to taste with salt and pepper.

Season the ragu again, if needed, and serve it with the polenta, drizzled with a glug of olive oil.

Make it vegan
Swap regular milk for dairy-free milk.

SAAG ALOO SAMOSAS

This recipe should totally be famous. It works perfectly – my favourite side dish inside my other favourite side dish!

To make 4 samosas

1 potato, diced

200g frozen spinach

1 tsp curry powder

2 sheets of filo pastry

2 tbsp mango chutney

Olive oil

Salt and pepper

To cook

Season and pan-fry the diced potato in a splash of olive oil over a medium heat for about 10 minutes until it starts to soften, then add the frozen spinach and a teaspoon of curry powder. Continue to cook so the spinach defrosts. Once defrosted, season to taste and set to one side to cool.

Preheat your oven to 190°C/gas mark 5.

Cut both filo sheets in half lengthways so you have 4 pieces of filo.

Take one piece of filo and fold it in half lengthways. Fold one of the corners over to make a triangle at one end. Then fold along the side of the triangle to create a pocket (you might have to watch my YouTube video on how to do this). Fill the pocket with a tablespoon of the potato and spinach mixture, then fold over the excess filo to cover the filling and make a neat triangle.

Repeat with the remaining pieces of filo, so you end up with 4 samosas. Then lightly brush the samosas with olive oil and bake in the oven for about 20 minutes until golden brown.

Serve warm with the mango chutney.

BELL PEPPER JALFREZI

This is how to show off a vegetable curry. There's no hiding behind a sauce here, so the vibrancy of these spectacularly colourful peppers really shines through.

To make 1 portion

2 tbsp tomato purée

Splash of sesame oil

1 tsp curry powder

Pinch of dried chilli flakes

1 garlic clove, sliced

½ onion, sliced

¼ red pepper, sliced

¼ yellow pepper, sliced

¼ green pepper, sliced

½ vegetable stock cube

Salt and pepper

To cook

Start by pan-frying the tomato purée in a splash of sesame oil along with the curry powder, chilli flakes and garlic over a medium heat. After about 2 minutes, add the onion and peppers and continue to fry for a few more minutes before crumbling in half a stock cube and adding a splash more sesame oil. Fry for a final minute, while stirring, season to taste and serve.

INDEX

A

apple & stilton slaw **144**

asparagus: vegetable terrine **166**

aubergines: aubergine milanese **76**

    aubergine pangrattato **190**

    aubergine parmigiana **160**

    aubergine pho **170**

    aubergine ragu & polenta **194**

    aubergine thermidor **130**

    black bean moussaka **96**

    caponata **110**

    harissa-baked aubergine **148**

    polenta-crusted aubergine **182**

B

balti veg pie **192**

bean sprouts: spicy chilli bean sprouts **172**

beans *see* black beans; cannellini beans; green beans; kidney beans

beetroot latkes **116**

biryani: onion biryani **36**

black beans: black bean & chilli enchiladas **22**

    black bean moussaka **96**

    cashews in black bean sauce **114**

blinis **132**

bread: polenta cornbread **52**

    potato focaccia **72**

    roasted panzanella **34**

    see also toast

breadcrumbs: aubergine pangrattato **190**

    charred peppers & breadcrumbs **134**

    portobello Kiev **146**

broccoli: filo bianco **174**

    Thai-style red curry noodles **118**

bulgur wheat: hot tabbouleh **150**

    roasted butternut squash & bulgur wheat **26**

burgers: portobello stilton burger **66**

butternut squash: butternut squash polenta **156**

    roasted butternut squash & bulgur wheat **26**

C

cabbage: cabbage potstickers **102**

    griddled cabbage chop & lentils **42**

    nasi goreng **30**

    pulled BBQ mushrooms **98**

cacio e pepe **56**

Caesar salad **184**

cannellini beans with leek & tomatoes **54**

caponata **110**

carrots: carrot & coriander salad **106**

    chunky balti veg pie **192**

    pulled BBQ mushrooms **98**

    vegetable Cornish pasty **40**

    vegetable hash **18**

cashews in black bean sauce **114**

cauliflower: cauliflower 3 ways **86**

    cauliflower tacos **78**

chana masala **138**

Cheddar cheese: cheese soufflé omelette **112**

    filo bianco **174**

    potato & leek slice **82**

    Welsh rarebit & tomato pie **136**

cheese: leek & blue cheese tart **108**

    see also Cheddar cheese; cream cheese; feta; goat's cheese; halloumi; mozzarella; Parmesan cheese; ricotta; stilton

chickpeas: chana masala **138**

    chickpea & saag mash **142**

    coconut daal **162**

    coronation chickpeas **94**

    roast chickpea gyros **44**

chilli: vegan lentil chilli **38**

chillies: black bean & chilli enchiladas **22**

    spicy chilli bean sprouts **172**

chimichurri **60**

Chinese-style oyster mushrooms **84**

ciabatta: roasted panzanella **34**

coconut milk: coconut daal **162**

    Thai-style red curry noodles **118**

coriander: carrot & coriander salad **106**

corn on the cob **154**

cornbread **52**

Cornish pasty **40**

coronation chickpeas **94**

courgettes: chunky balti veg pie **192**

    fried tomatoes & courgettes **180**

    griddled vegetable couscous **88**

    vegetable hash **18**

    vegetable terrine **166**

couscous: caponata **110**

griddled vegetable couscous 88

cream cheese: vegetable terrine 166

curry: bell pepper jalfrezi 198

    chana masala 138

    chickpea & saag mash 142

    chunky balti veg pie 192

    coconut daal 162

    coronation chickpeas 94

    green bean & lentil curry 62

    halloumi saag 92

    halloumi tikka masala 120

    Thai-style red curry noodles 118

D

daal: coconut daal 162

dumplings: cabbage potstickers 102

E

eggs: blinis 132

    caramelised onion quiche 158

    cheese soufflé omelette 112

    French toast 16

    green bean & lentil salad 24

    homemade pasta 70

    pizza frittata 168

    vegetable hash 18

enchiladas: black bean & chilli enchiladas 22

F

falafel: pea falafel 64

feta: feta goujons 74

    pea, mint & feta salad 80

roasted butternut squash & bulgur wheat 26

filo pastry: filo bianco 174

    saag aloo samosas 196

focaccia: potato focaccia 72

French toast 16

frittata: pizza frittata 168

G

goat's cheese: messy pea lasagne 50

goujons: feta goujons 74

green beans: green bean & lentil curry 62

    green bean & lentil salad 24

gyros: roast chickpea gyros 44

H

halloumi: halloumi bake 186

    halloumi saag 92

    halloumi tikka masala 120

harissa: harissa-baked aubergine 148

hash: vegetable hash 18

J

jalfrezi: bell pepper jalfrezi 198

jollof rice 68

K

kidney beans: vegan lentil chilli 38

L

lasagne: leek & spinach lasagne 48

    messy pea lasagne 50

    rotolo 176

latkes: beetroot latkes 116

leeks: cannellini beans with leek & tomatoes 54

    leek & blue cheese tart 108

    leek & mushroom pot pie 128

    leek & spinach lasagne 48

    potato & leek slice 82

    yaki soba 90

lentils: coconut daal 162

    green bean & lentil curry 62

    green bean & lentil salad 24

    griddled cabbage chop & lentils 42

    lentil soup 104

    vegan lentil chilli 38

M

milk risotto 188

mint: pea, mint & feta salad 80

moussaka: black bean moussaka 96

mozzarella: pizza frittata 168

puttanesca bake 164

mushrooms: Chinese-style oyster mushrooms 84

    leek & mushroom pot pie 128

    mushroom stroganoff 126

    portobello Kiev 146

    portobello stilton burger 66

    pulled BBQ mushrooms 98

N

nasi goreng 30

noodles: aubergine pho 170

    Thai-style red curry noodles 118

    yaki soba 90

O

omelette: cheese soufflé omelette 112

onions: caramelised onion quiche 158

    griddled vegetable couscous 88

    onion biryani 36

    see also spring onions

orecchiette: spinach orecchiette 122

P

pancakes: beetroot latkes 116

    blinis 132

panzanella 34

Parmesan cheese: aubergine parmigiana 160

    cacio e pepe 56

    peas, pasta & cream 46

pasta: aubergine milanese 76

    aubergine pangrattato 190

    cacio e pepe 56

    homemade pasta 70

    leek & spinach lasagne 48

    messy pea lasagne 50

    peas, pasta & cream 46

    puttanesca bake 164

    rotolo 176

    spinach orecchiette 122

pasties: vegetable Cornish pasty 40

patatas bravas 20

peas: messy pea lasagne 50

    pea falafel 64

    pea, mint & feta salad 80

    peas, pasta & cream 46

peperonata sweet potatoes 124

peppers: bell pepper jalfrezi 198

    charred peppers & breadcrumbs 134

    griddled vegetable couscous 88

    hot tabbouleh 150

    sweet & sour peppers 32

peppers (roasted): peperonata sweet potatoes 124

    spicy patatas bravas 20

    vegetable terrine 166

pho: aubergine pho 170

pineapple fried rice 140

pizza frittata 168

polenta: aubergine ragu & polenta 194

    butternut squash polenta 156

    polenta cornbread 52

    polenta-crusted aubergine 182

portobello mushrooms: mushroom stroganoff 126

    portobello Kiev 146

    portobello stilton burger 66

    pulled BBQ mushrooms 98

potatoes: blinis 132

    chickpea & saag mash 142

    chunky balti veg pie 192

    crispy potato Caesar salad 184

    green bean & lentil salad 24

    portobello Kiev 146

    portobello stilton burger 66

potato & leek slice 82

potato focaccia 72

saag aloo samosas 196

spicy patatas bravas 20

vegetable Cornish pasty 40

vegetable hash 18

vegetable terrine 166

potstickers 102

puff pastry: leek & blue cheese tart 108

    leek & mushroom pot pie 128

    potato & leek slice 82

pulled BBQ mushrooms 98

puttanesca bake 164

Q

quiche: caramelised onion quiche 158

R

ragu: aubergine ragu & polenta 194

rice: jollof rice 68

rice (arborio): milk risotto 188

rice (basmati): black bean & chilli enchiladas 22

    Chinese-style oyster mushrooms 84

    coronation chickpeas 94

    onion biryani 36

    sweet & sour peppers 32

    vegan lentil chilli 38

rice (brown): mushroom stroganoff 126

    nasi goreng 30

    pineapple fried rice 140

ricotta: rotolo **176**

risotto: milk risotto **188**

rotolo **176**

S

saag aloo samosas **196**

salads: carrot & coriander salad **106**

crispy potato Caesar salad **184**

green bean & lentil salad **24**

griddled sweet potato **60**

pea, mint & feta salad **80**

roasted panzanella **34**

see also slaw

samosas: saag aloo samosas **196**

shortcrust pastry: caramelised onion quiche **158**

vegetable Cornish pasty **40**

slaw: apple & stilton slaw **144**

pulled BBQ mushrooms **98**

soufflé: cheese soufflé omelette **112**

soup: aubergine pho **170**

lentil soup **104**

spaghetti: aubergine milanese **76**

cacio e pepe **56**

spinach: chickpea & saag mash **142**

halloumi saag **92**

leek & spinach lasagne **48**

pea falafel **64**

rotolo **176**

saag aloo samosas **196**

spinach orecchiette **122**

spring onions: hot tabbouleh **150**

squash *see* butternut squash

sriracha: Thai-style red curry noodles **118**

stilton: apple & stilton slaw **144**

portobello stilton burger **66**

stroganoff: mushroom stroganoff **126**

sweet & sour peppers **32**

sweet potatoes: griddled sweet potato **60**

peperonata sweet potatoes **124**

pulled BBQ mushrooms **98**

sweetcorn bisque **28**

T

tabbouleh **150**

tacos: cauliflower tacos **78**

Tenderstem broccoli: filo bianco **174**

terrine: vegetable terrine **166**

Thai-style red curry noodles **118**

tikka masala **120**

toast: French toast **16**

tomatoes: fried tomatoes & courgettes **180**

Welsh rarebit & tomato pie **136**

tomatoes (cherry): cannellini beans with leek & tomatoes **54**

roasted panzanella **34**

tomatoes (sun-dried): pizza frittata **168**

tomatoes (tinned): aubergine parmigiana **160**

aubergine ragu & polenta **194**

black bean moussaka **96**

chana masala **138**

chunky balti veg pie **192**

halloumi bake **186**

halloumi tikka masala **120**

harissa-baked aubergine **148**

jollof rice **68**

puttanesca bake **164**

sweetcorn bisque **28**

tortillas: cauliflower tacos **78**

W

Welsh rarebit & tomato pie **136**

Y

yaki soba **90**

First published in 2019 by Headline Home
an imprint of Headline Publishing Group

1

Cataloguing in Publication Data is available from
the British Library

ISBN 978 1 4722 6407 7
eISBN 978 1 4722 6406 0

Publishing Director: Lindsey Evans
Senior Editor: Kate Miles
Art Direction and Design: Superfantastic
Photography: Dan Jones
Home Economist Assistants: Sophie Garwood and Grace Paul
Copy Editors: Laura Nickoll and Sophie Elletson
Page Makeup: EM&EN
Proofreader: Ilona Jasiewicz
Indexer: Caroline Wilding

Printed and bound in Germany by Mohn Media
Colour reproduction by Alta Image
Typeset in Brandon Grotesque, Avenir, Billabong

Headline's policy is to use papers that are natural,
renewable and recyclable products and made from wood
grown in sustainable forests. The logging and manufacturing
processes are expected to conform to the environmental
regulations of the country of origin.

HEADLINE PUBLISHING GROUP
An Hachette UK Company
Carmelite House
50 Victoria Embankment
London EC4Y 0DZ

www.headline.co.uk
www.hachette.co.uk